THE NORTH ATLANTIC FRONT

THE NORTH ATLANTIC FRONT

Orkney, Shetland, Faroe and Iceland at War

James Miller

Birlinn

Frontispiece.

In the winter of 1942–43, seamen clear ice from the foredeck of HMS Scylla. *(Copyright IWM. No. A 15365)*

This edition published in 2005 by
Birlinn Limited
West Newington House
10 Newington Road
Edinburgh
EH9 1QS

www.birlinn.co.uk

British Library Cataloguing-in-Publication Data
A catalogue record for this book is available from the British Library

Layout and page make up: Mark Blackadder

Printed and bound in Great Britain by the Bath Press, Glasgow

PREFACE

The term 'North Atlantic Front' seems never to have been used officially but the British strategy in both World Wars, in 1914–18 and 1939–45, of trying to confine German naval activity did create a 'front' in practice. In the trackless ocean, the front materialised only as the protagonists' ships and aircraft, and as the land masses where one flag or another could be raised. In the First World War the Grand Fleet based at Scapa Flow and the Northern Patrol operating from Swarbacks Minn gave the front tangible form. In 1918 it became briefly and more precisely defined by the laying of a great minefield from Orkney to Norway. The German occupation of Norway in 1940 blasted aside Britain's intention to repeat this strategy in the Second World War and, outflanked, the front retreated westwards and was re-established along the Shetland–Faroes–Iceland chain.

The idea for this text grew out of an earlier book *Scapa* about the Royal Navy's great base in Orkney. In this volume the focus shifts from Scapa Flow to the other places in the north that made up the North Atlantic front. The two books complement each other and share an approach, combining photographs with material from official reports, eyewitness accounts and contemporary writings. Pressures of time and space have ensured that the story is told largely from a British point of view, and I hope that our neighbours in Norway, the Faroes, Iceland and Germany will forgive this. It is also essentially a story of war at sea, of a conflict between ships, aircraft and their crews, but this is not meant to downplay the role of the many thousands who served in the land garrisons defending the islands.

The spelling of Scandinavian place names varies considerably in British sources, especially in wartime documents when harassed officers and clerks had to wrestle with unfamiliar words for the first time. By and large I have standardised spellings according to how names appear on modern maps but have retained the ending '-fjord' instead of the Faroese and Icelandic *-fjörður* as the former is easier for readers of English. I have also adopted the conventional renditions of Althing, for the name of Iceland's Parliament, the *Alþing*, and Thorshavn for *Tórshavn*.

I am grateful to many people for their assistance with the research for this book. Much valuable material was found in Aberdeen University Library, the Imperial War Museum Photograph Archive, Inverness Library, Orkney Public Library, and the Public Record Office. Without the assistance of Brian Smith and Angus Johnson in the Shetland Archives, Douglas Garden and his staff in the Shetland Library, and Tommy Watt and his staff at the Shetland Museum, my job would have taken much longer and been more difficult. Scalloway Museum is an essential stop for anyone interested in the Shetland Bus.

I am also indebted to Thomas Smyth, the archivist of the Black Watch, CSgt W.T. Turner of the Staffordshire Regiment Museum, Mrs P. Boyd at the HQ of the Prince of Wales's Own Regiment of Yorkshire, Sharon Martin of South Lanarkshire Council for information about the Cameronians, and Lt Col (Retd) A.M. Cumming OBE for information on the 7th Seaforth Highlanders. Roddie Campbell was generous with his memories of his time as a Lovat Scout trooper in the Faroes.

Robert and Nora Manson could not have been better hosts during my stay in Lerwick, and not only looked after an itinerant writer but took an active interest in his work. Robert also generously allowed the use of his father's written memoir.

Dr Michael Barnes of University College London, Rhona Campbell in Dingwall, Bert Stenning in Brighton, Maureen Venzi in Calgary, and Lorna Hunter of the Northern Lighthouse Board were all generous in responding to specific queries. James Neale kindly allowed me to use his father's photographs and David Hanson his compilation of aircraft incidents in Shetland in the Second World War.

Once again I am indebted to my agent, Duncan McAra, and Dick Raynor for help with photographs.

PICTURE CREDITS

The sources for the illustrations are given with the individual captions. I would particularly like to thank the staffs of the Imperial War Museum (IWM) and the Public Record Office (PRO) for their help in finding images; these pictures are all Crown Copyright. I also wish to thank the staffs of Shetland Museum and Orkney Library for their help in searching through their extensive picture collections; Vidar and Dorothy Olsen for their assistance in dealing with the Norges Hjemmefront Museum; Roddie Campbell and Robert Manson for their kindness in allowing use of their own pictures; and *The Yorkshire Post* and Mrs P. Boyd of the Prince of Wales Own Regiment of Yorkshire Museum for the pictures from the wartime publication *Garrison in Iceland*. Every reasonable effort was made to trace the owners of copyright in each image.

Abbreviations

Some less well-known abbreviations used in the text

AMC	armed merchant cruiser
DSC	Distinguished Service Cross
ENSA	Entertainments National Service Association
GOC	General Officer Commanding
NAAFI	Navy Army and Air Force Institutes
RDF	radio direction finding
RNVR	Royal Navy Volunteer Reserve
Toc H	Christian fellowship movement for service personnel

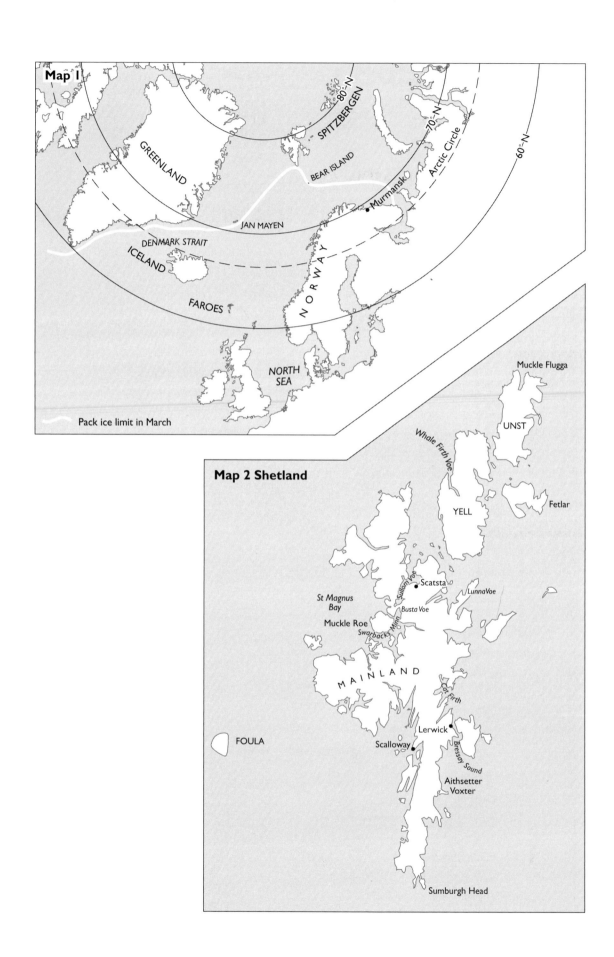

Map I

80° N

SPITZBERGEN

GREENLAND

BEAR ISLAND

70° N

Arctic Circle

JAN MAYEN

Murmansk

DENMARK STRAIT

60° N

ICELAND

NORWAY

FAROES

NORTH
SEA

Pack ice limit in March

Map 2 Shetland

Muckle Flugga

Whale Firth Voe

UNST

YELL

Fetlar

Sullom Voe

Scatsta

LunnaVoe

St Magnus
Bay

Busta Voe

Muckle Roe

Swarbacks Minn

MAINLAND

Cat Firth

Lerwick

FOULA

Scalloway

Bressay Sound

Aithsetter
Voxter

Sumburgh Head

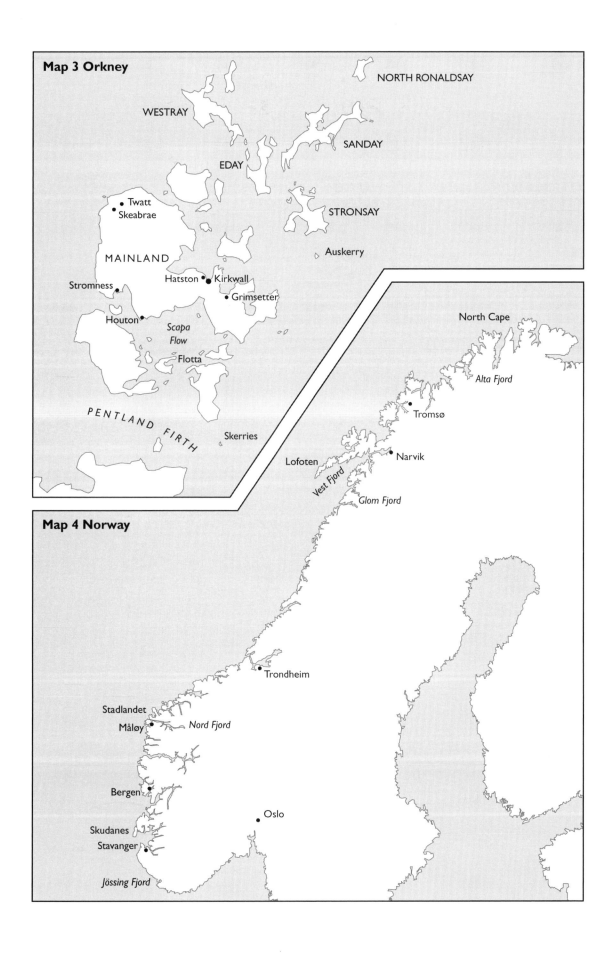

Map 3 Orkney

NORTH RONALDSAY

WESTRAY

SANDAY

EDAY

STRONSAY

Twatt
Skeabrae

MAINLAND

Auskerry

Stromness

Hatston • Kirkwall

Grimsetter

Houton

Scapa Flow

Flotta

PENTLAND FIRTH

Skerries

Map 4 Norway

North Cape

Alta Fjord

Tromsø

Lofoten

Narvik

Vest Fjord

Glom Fjord

Trondheim

Stadlandet

Måløy • *Nord Fjord*

Bergen

Oslo

Skudanes

Stavanger

Jössing Fjord

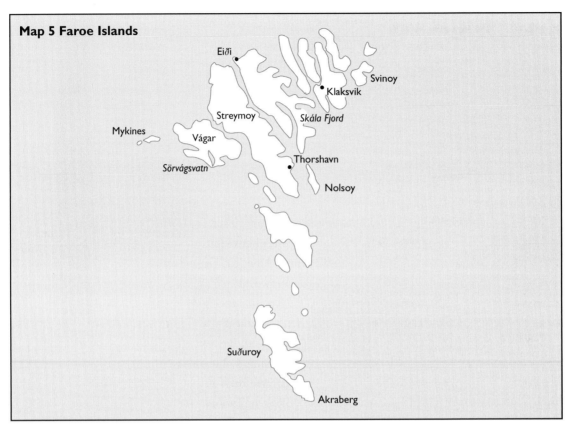

Map 5 Faroe Islands

Eiði

Svinoy

Klaksvik

Skála Fjord

Streymoy

Mykines

Vágar

Thorshavn

Sörvágsvatn

Nolsoy

Suðuroy

Akraberg

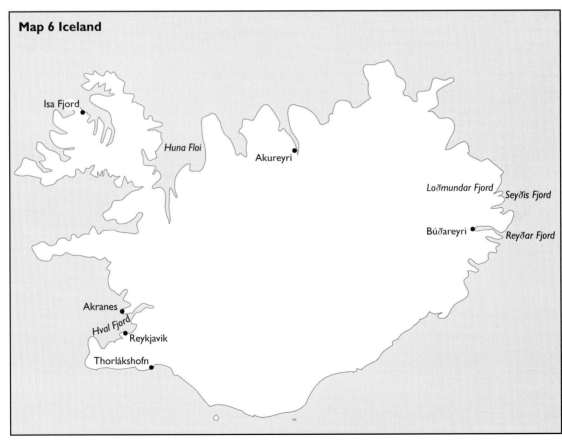

Map 6 Iceland

Isa Fjord

Huna Floi

Akureyri

Loðmundar Fjord

Seyðis Fjord

Búðareyri

Reyðar Fjord

Akranes

Hval Fjord

Reykjavik

Thorlákshofn

THE NORTH ATLANTIC FRONT

A glance at the map of the North Atlantic shows a series of islands and island groups lying like stepping stones between the northern British mainland, Scandinavia and North America. First comes Orkney and then Shetland, with Fair Isle snugly between them. The distance between Lerwick and Bergen is about 220 miles. Around 200 miles north-west of Shetland, the Faroes rise precipitously from the ocean, and another hop of 200 miles brings one to the eastern tip of Iceland. Beyond Iceland and the Denmark Strait lies the forbidding shore of Greenland. Throughout most of recorded European history the northern islands have been regarded as lying on the periphery, far from the centres of power and population, shores beset with fierce weather and cursed with barren soils. In the twentieth century, however, the inhabitants of these islands found themselves living in maritime fortresses on the front line between contested areas of sea.

There are similarities between the island groups but also some important distinctions: Orkney has broad acres of fertile land whereas the barren Shetland ground has made the islanders more dependent on the sea. On the eve of the First World War the population of Shetland numbered around 28,000, that of Orkney about 25,000. The Faroes, with around 18,000 inhabitants in 1914, rise from the Atlantic in steep-sided splendour but are almost critically short of arable ground, making the population again dependent on the sea for survival: sea birds and whale meat were prominent features of the traditional diet. In 1914 the Faroes constituted a province of Denmark and were administered by an *amtmand*, or governor, and a provincial parliament, the *Løgting*.[1] Some strong trade links had developed between the Faroese and their southern neighbours in Shetland during the nineteenth century, and scholars had begun to explore the islanders' common Scandinavian heritage.

Just before the First World War, Britain was in danger of losing the total superiority as a maritime power that she had gained after the defeat of the French and Spanish fleets during the wars against Napoleon. France, Italy, Russia, Germany, Japan and the United States had all built dreadnoughts, the

Fig. 1
*The German fleet
anchored in Bressay Sound
off Lerwick in July 1904.
(Shetland Museum)*

giant battleships that took their general name from the first of the kind, the British HMS *Dreadnought*, commissioned in 1906. Along with the revolution in warship design and the appearance of such new weapons as the torpedo and the sea-mine had come a readjustment of European power politics. France was now the ally of Britain, and the most probable enemy was Germany, ruled by Kaiser Wilhelm II, the cousin of King George V.

Germany had built an impressive fleet by the early 1900s and an arms race in battleship construction developed between her and Britain. Both countries used their ships to show the flag and impress their neighbours. In the form of a squadron of nine ships, the Kaiser's new and mighty sea arm made its first official visit to Shetland in May 1900, but, in July 1904, it steamed into Bressay Sound and anchored off Lerwick in a much more impressive array, the ironclad battlewagons a striking contrast to the ranks of steam drifters assembled for the summer herring fishing. On 23 July the *Shetland Times* noted that the thirty-two battleships, cruisers and torpedo-boats formed the biggest fleet that Germany had yet sent to foreign waters and proceeded to give statistics for each vessel: for example, the flagship *Kaiser Wilhelm II* was 377 feet long and 11,130 tons, carried 9.4-inch guns and was capable of 18 knots. A week later, the editor of the *Shetland Times* printed some further thoughts about the event:

> The fact that in the present Active Fleet there is only one of the ships which were here four years ago emphasises the up-to-date character of the German navy as kept up by the ambitious energy of the Kaiser … Shetlanders would rather that the thanks [for the spectacle] had been due to our own Navy than to that of a continental power whose ways have not always been our ways; and while they can fully appreciate the quiet and most creditable behaviour on shore of the German bluejacket they cannot after all forget that, with all his little failings, 'Jack's the boy'.[2]

The newspaper went on to remind its readers that it had been twenty-one years since the British fleet had been seen in Shetland waters. The Admiralty seemed strangely reluctant to respond to invitations to send ships of the Royal Navy to Shetland, despite the fact that the islands had the second-largest Royal Naval Reserve training station in the country. It was now possible, in the editor's opinion, that the *Admiralstab*, the German naval staff, knew more about the Shetland coast than did the Admiralty in London.

Perhaps some of this comment pricked a conscience in the Admiralty for, two months later, some ships of the Channel Fleet, under Vice-Admiral Lord

Charles Beresford in the cruiser HMS *Caesar*, visited Lerwick. But it was too little too late, as far as the doughty editor of the *Shetland Times* was concerned. First fifteen ships had been expected, then eleven, and finally only four had appeared. In an orotund editorial dripping in sarcasm, the editor vented his feelings: 'the people of Lerwick have from time to time heard of the Channel Fleet and ... that it was on its way to pay them a visit but not having yet been convinced by optical evidence of its actual existence they are inclined to be in some dubiety as to its actuality'. He dismissed the excuse that the anchorage was not suitable for battleships by suggesting that a polite request to the German authorities might produce all the information the Admiralty obviously lacked.[3]

These feelings did not prevent the islanders from showing hospitality to the sailors, but the airing of them in the newspaper may have lain behind the fact that on the eve of the First World War some officers in the Admiralty began to express concern that the courtesy calls to Shetland by German warships may have eroded the Shetlanders' 'sense of British nationality' and opened a weak spot in Britain's defences.[4] This somewhat extraordinary fear punches home how much strategic thinking on naval matters had changed since the advent of the dreadnought, as well as revealing how little was really known in London about the northern islands.

There was apparently no similar concern entertained about the inhabitants of Orkney, where the Royal Navy was laying the foundations for its principal base in Scapa Flow, a sheltered basin ringed by protecting islands. But the Navy was more familiar with Orkney: it had been calling at Kirkwall for many years, and had been anchoring in Scapa Flow since 1909 on elaborate and extensive exercises. The Scapa Flow base became the hinge on which swung the maritime front extending through the northern island groups. Its story, however, has been told already and it will not figure strongly in this narrative.[5] Although the Orcadians were well disposed towards the Navy, some of them nevertheless found the attitude of some officers difficult to swallow. The visitors had to learn that the inhabitants of these far-flung parts of Britain were not the country bumpkins they may have taken them to be but were often better educated and more aware of the world than their southern neighbours. For centuries the northern islands had been a maritime crossroads. For example, Orcadians made up at one point the great majority of the employees of the Hudson's Bay Company, and Shetlanders were prominent among the crews of the merchant navy.

British naval strategy in the First World War was based on bottling up German naval strength in the North Sea. The southern exit through the

Fig. 2

A flotilla of Royal Navy torpedo boats (early destroyers) in Kirkwall Bay in August 1906. (Orkney Library, David Horne Collection)

Fig. 3

Ships of the combined Home and Atlantic Fleets in Scapa Flow in April 1910. (Orkney Library, Tom Kent Collection)

HOME AND ATLANTIC FLEETS. SCAPA FLOW. 28TH APL.1910 IKENT 2.

English Channel narrowed to an easily guarded twenty-one miles between Dover and Calais. (The French navy was also well placed to share the patrolling of the Channel with the Royal Navy.) It was much more likely that a German break-out would be ventured through the wide gap between the northern parts of Britain and the Norwegian coast. And this put the northern islands in the front line.

Rear-Admiral David Beatty summed up the strategic situation for Winston Churchill in April 1912 some six months after the latter had become First Lord of the Admiralty: '…with a proper distribution of her fleets, Great Britain is capable of confining all or nearly all warlike operations within the North Sea'.[6] It was obvious that, to thwart this strategy, Germany might try to seize an anchorage on the Norwegian coast or even in the northern isles themselves. In the following two years, as war became inevitable, the naval commands on both sides of the North Sea began to move their capital ships and prepare for advantage for whenever the trumpet should finally sound. There was some debate in the Admiralty over whether Rosyth, Invergordon or Scapa Flow should be made the main base for the Grand Fleet before Scapa Flow was settled upon as the best anchorage.

After the War, Lord John 'Jackie' Fisher, who as First Sea Lord had pushed through the development of the dreadnought and dragged the somewhat stuffy Edwardian Royal Navy by the scruff of the neck into a more modern era, tried to take the credit for picking Scapa Flow. In an article in *The Times*, published in September 1919, he wrote:

> Once looking at a chart in my secluded room at the Admiralty in 1905, I saw a large inland land-locked sheet of water unsurveyed and nameless … One hour after I thus gazed on the chart an Admiralty surveying vessel was en route there … No one, however talented, except myself could explain how, playing with a pair of compasses, I took the German fleet as the centre for one leg … and swept the chart with the other leg to find a place for our Fleet beyond practicability of surprise by the Germans. The Fleet was there at Scapa Flow before the War broke out.[7]

The old seadog, who had made plenty of enemies during his time in power, was not to be let off with this outrageous claim, and he was lampooned in a rewording of Hymn 364 which began 'Praise Jack from whom all Scapas flow'.

When hostilities began on 4 August 1914, the Grand Fleet was indeed occupying the Flow. In the last days of July the Royal Navy, in the form of a

Fig. 4

The destroyer HMS Itchen went ashore at the Head of Work, near Kirkwall, during a night exercise before the First World War. (Orkney Library)

light cruiser and four destroyers, had already established a presence in Shetland, just in case the Germans were thinking of making a move to grab the northern islands. The Admiralty contacted its new Commander-in-Chief of the Grand Fleet, Admiral Sir John Jellicoe, with a report that Germany had established a base in Norway at 62°N (north of Bergen). Naval intelligence was confident that no German ships had entered Norwegian waters before midnight on 5 August but Jellicoe sent the 3rd Cruiser Squadron, supported by a flotilla of twenty destroyers, to scout the Norwegian coast.[8] Other ships were despatched to Shetland and to watch the Fair Isle Channel. Jellicoe also requested the Admiralty confirm that Germany had not occupied the Faroes and sent cruisers north to check if anything was afoot there. The scouting cruisers found that no German vessels, apart from fishing boats, had called at the Faroes in the last two years. On 11 August Jellicoe told the Admiralty that nothing suspicious had been found at Skudanes, near Stavanger, and asked for a formal apology to be made to the Norwegian government for the Royal Navy's infringement of their territorial waters.

Norway, like all the Scandinavian countries, remained neutral throughout the First World War and was to make frequent protests against belligerent ships making use of her long coastline. However, the Inner Leads, a channel

of sheltered water lying between the hundreds of offshore islands and the main Norwegian coast with its deep, sheltered fjords indenting the shore all the way from Stavanger to the North Cape, offered many hiding places too tempting to resist. Jellicoe was sure that German U-boats and merchant ships were using them in their attempts to slip past his forces but the Admiralty beseeched him not to offend the Norwegians more than he could help. In July 1915 he protested to Beatty, then in command of the British battle-cruisers stationed at Rosyth, that the Navy was 'trying to make war with gloves on, and I am being harried because the trawler I have on the Norwegian coast which bagged a German merchant ship the other day possibly made a mistake of 100 yards about territorial waters. But I am sending over 5 more with indifferent navigating appliances !! so there may be more errors of the same nature.'[9]

On the day the war began, Rear-Admiral Dudley R.S. de Chair was sailing northwards along the west coast of England aboard HMS *Crescent,* on his way to command what was to become a very effective weapon against the German nation. Up until a couple of months before this, de Chair had been desk-bound in the Admiralty as Churchill's naval secretary, but then the orders had been issued for him to take command of a training squadron and

Fig. 5

A line of Orion-class battleships of the Grand Fleet pass south through Hoxa Sound from Scapa Flow. (Copyright IWM. No. Q 102267)

Fig. 6

*A mixed force of officers
and ranks at Stanger Head
on Flotta.
(Orkney Library)*

Fig. 7

A naval gun crew on the island of Auskerry in the First World War. (Orkney Library)

hoist his flag in the *Crescent*. The latter was a cruiser, already an old ship, a reminder of the old pre-dreadnought days, having been built in the early 1890s along with the seven others in her class, collectively known as the Edgars after one of their number, HMS *Edgar*. They were armed with 9.2-inch and 6-inch guns and were powered by coal-fired engines that pushed them along at a maximum of 17 knots.[10] As the *Crescent* passed the Welsh coast, de Chair sent wireless messages to her sister ships in Plymouth, Portsmouth and Queenstown to follow him north. The ageing cruisers now shed all pretence of being a training squadron – that had been a cover all along – and adopted their intended role as the 10th Cruiser Squadron implementing the Northern Patrol and intercepting any ships bound for Germany.

The patrol took its first prize on the following morning, 4 August, near the Mull of Kintyre when HMS *Grafton* fired a shot across the bows of the *Wilhelm Behrens*, a German steamer with a cargo of timber, put a prize crew aboard her and sent her into confinement on the Clyde. De Chair's squadron carried on north to Scapa Flow, where they waited for all their members to gather and prepared for long patrols in the stormy waters to the north. Communications could be difficult in 1914, when many ships still did not carry a wireless set, and the crews of the two German sailing trawlers that the patrol captured north-east of Shetland on 8 August did not even know that the war had begun. The fishermen were taken prisoner and their vessels were sent to the bottom. In this period, some British fishing boats were taken by German warships in a similar fashion. The people on Foula didn't learn of the outbreak of the war until the 10th, as the weekly mailboat had been delayed by bad weather.

De Chair was to enjoy a high measure of independence in his command of the Northern Patrol, but in the early months he had to answer various calls for assistance from Jellicoe at Scapa Flow, where the Commander-in-Chief was desperately trying to keep his fleet intact while ascertaining what the enemy was likely to attempt. The defences of Scapa Flow were not yet adequate to protect the anchorage against what Jellicoe feared – lightning surprise attacks by destroyers or submarines – and the Grand Fleet spent a great deal of time in the relative safety of the open sea, burning fuel by the ton and depriving crews of total rest. On 18 August Jellicoe asked de Chair to station three of his ships off the Norwegian coast at Nordfjord to intercept any enemy vessels trying to slip through the Inner Leads. An armed merchant cruiser, the *Kaiser Wilhelm der Grosse*, had already escaped this way on 5 August and had skirted the north coast of Iceland on her way to attack British shipping in the Atlantic. Jellicoe also called on the cruisers of the Northern Patrol to guard the northern flank of the Grand Fleet whenever it made a sweep into the North Sea until the Admiralty reminded him that this was not their real purpose.

The blockade imposed on German commerce by the Northern Patrol was governed by a set of regulations drawn up by the British government at the start of the war. On 4 August a Royal Proclamation declared that goods were to be listed as either Absolute Contraband – any weapons, explosives or war materials – or Conditional Contraband – in practice, almost everything else, including foodstuffs and vehicles, that could have a military use. Trade between Britain and Germany was of course forbidden, but the carrying of goods from Britain to any northern European port was also subject to the regulations. The sale of British-mined coal was carefully regulated with a knock-on effect on merchant shipping sailing between European ports. On 20 August a British Order-in-Council, which became known as the Declaration of London, set up a prize court to handle seized ships and goods and decide what was to be done with them. The Declaration of London was soon challenged as being against international law, as the ships of neutral nations were also stopped, searched and often seized.

The war began in Shetland with the mobilization of the men of the Royal Naval Reserve (RNR), while in Orkney the members of the Royal Garrison

Artillery (Territorial Force) had already begun to man their defence stations. On Sunday 2 August the word had gone out for all the Shetland reservists to report to their headquarters in Lerwick, at the Customs House, but it took some time for the summons to reach the northern islands. On the following day the *Shetland Times* noted that the streets were thronged: 'The men formed quite a jovial crowd and joked and chaffed all around; but the women were in quite an opposite mood.' The editor published his thoughts about the historic occasion: 'There are times when Shetland feels itself no small section of the British Empire and Monday was one of those occasions … It was as though some electrical current had stirred the whole community and the all-absorbing topic was war.'[11] The men of the Shetland RNR had enrolled on the understanding that they would not be called on to serve outside their own islands but, when the Navy appealed for volunteers for the Fleet, they all, to a man, came forward. Some 800 were accepted and the remainder were retained to serve locally.[12] As the men of the RNR assembled in Lerwick, the members of the Shetland companies of the Gordon Highlanders (Territorial Force) had also been summoned; some of them were detailed to guard the telegraph cable huts around the islands and, in time, many would be sent to join the troops in France and other overseas theatres. Shetland also furnished some 3,000 men for the merchant marine.

On 7 August 1914 Parliament passed the Defence of the Realm Act. This first version of DORA, as the act came to be called, was soon extended, amended and otherwise changed to provide the legal and military authorities with an almost draconian set of powers aimed at securing the country's defence: vehicles could be stopped and searched; pub opening hours were severely curtailed; the keeping of carrier pigeons was restricted; people could be ordered to stay indoors, or outside a certain locality; and the Army and Navy could commandeer practically anything. Offenders were liable for court martial and anyone found guilty of 'assisting the enemy' could find himself before a firing squad. As the home of the Grand Fleet, Orkney was particularly targeted: 'No person shall land or embark at any port in the Orkney Islands' without permission of the Navy, ordered Herbert Samuel, the Secretary of State, in June 1916.[13] Shetland was treated in a similar fashion: the permission of an authorised naval officer was required before anyone could travel by sea between the islands. In October 1916 this regulation was applied to travel to and from Shetland as a whole. Passengers on inter-island steamers did not need individual permits, but the master had to keep a list of those aboard.

There were still a few sailing vessels trading in the islands, including a ketch from Unst called the *Silver Lining*. One of her skippers was a true salt called Daniel Dowell, a man who cared more about the sea than Admiralty regulations. One dark night during the war he was alone at the helm of the *Silver Lining*, his crew in their bunks, holding the ketch on a homeward course with a fair wind. As he was passing Fair Isle, a destroyer caught him in a searchlight beam and ordered him to follow her into Kirkwall. Dowell obediently put the wheel over and altered course. The Navy captain then realised that under sail and in this wind the *Silver Lining* could take days to reach Kirkwall and passed a towline to the ketch. Unfortunately the destroyer's power was too great and, before they had gone any distance, the strength of the hawser tore out the *Silver Lining*'s bit-heads. They made Kirkwall, however, and Dowell found himself, not for the first time, having to account for his presence underway at night in restricted waters. His explanation that a sailing vessel had to go with the wind, and his complaint about the damage to the *Silver Lining* were both accepted. The ketch was repaired at the Admiralty's expense and continued to sail.[14]

In the years before the outbreak of the war, the naval staffs on both sides of the North Sea were naturally extremely interested in what the opposing force might be up to, and took every opportunity to gather potentially useful information. Early in the period of British–German rivalry this could be attempted without much trouble, and no doubt, for example, the German minister of the interior who happened to be among the 200 passengers on the cruise liner *Oceana* when she called at Kirkwall in August 1906 and returned to Hamburg via Lerwick kept his eyes open.[15] It is, however, difficult to be certain of the extent of espionage, and conclusions about how much went on is clouded by the speculations of conspiracy theorists. Both World Wars have provided ample fodder for the latter: for example, it has been held that HMS *Vanguard*, the battleship that blew up in Scapa Flow in July 1917, was the victim of sabotage rather than an explosion of unstable ammunition; and that Lieutenant Gunther Prien's daring attack on HMS *Royal Oak* in October 1939 was carried out with the help of an agent on shore. Evidence in support of these views is conspicuously lacking. MI5, founded in 1909, had managed by 1914 to identify almost all the German agents in Britain and they were arrested on the eve of hostilities.[16]

Fears about espionage amounted at times almost to paranoia among some officers, and one unfortunate panic led to all the staff of the Lerwick Post Office being arrested on suspicion. This happened on Sunday 1 November 1914. Bystanders that day were surprised by the sight of postmen, office staff, cleaners and drivers being escorted to the jail by guards with fixed bayonets. The postmaster was summoned and, when he made his feelings about the ludicrous affair known, he too was promptly confined to a cell with his colleagues. The staff stayed behind bars for a week, where they organised a prolonged party of sorts, with records, books and food being sent in. Meanwhile no one was available to operate the cable link to Iceland and some of the staff, who happened to be members of the Territorial Force and therefore deemed to be slightly more above suspicion than the others, were released to fulfil this necessary duty. After a week the staff were all set free but no explanation for the extraordinary business was forthcoming. It later emerged that Admiralty dispatches en route from London to the 10th Cruiser Squadron headquarters had been mishandled, and suspicion had fallen on the Post Office until it was discovered that the mistake had been made by the Navy itself. The commanding officer of the Royal Marines, Lieutenant-Colonel H.C. Evans, who had drawn his revolver to cow the Post Office workers, was later transferred out of the islands.[17]

A man in Lerwick who had rigged wire on his roof to stop gulls gathering on it had to take it down as it looked too much like an aerial. The army asked the public in September 1914 to keep an eye out for airships. Usually, however, the authorities showed common sense and the islanders, well aware of the need for security, co-operated to the full. All the fishing boats in Shetland were listed and numbered, and only licensed boats, for example, could operate on the west side of the Mainland near Swarbacks Minn, the anchorage of the 10th Cruiser Squadron; so effective were some of these measures that many Shetlanders remained unaware of the Squadron's presence or purpose. The *Shetland Times* announced a few days after the outbreak of hostilities that it would publish no reports on the movement of ships or troops. In 1939 a similar security regime was to descend once more on Orkney and Shetland.

At the start of the war, Jellicoe had under his command in the Grand Fleet at Scapa Flow twenty-one dreadnoughts, eight pre-dreadnought battleships and four battlecruisers. Across the North Sea, at his bases on the short length of German coast between Holland and Denmark, Admiral Friedrich von Ingenohl, Jellicoe's opposite number and now his foe, led the High Seas Fleet with thirteen dreadnoughts, sixteen pre-dreadnoughts and five battlecruisers. With their large guns and towering size, these capital ships were expensive to build and maintain. They also symbolised the might of the nation and had been heavily promoted as such in the popular media; the loss of one was a blow to public morale as well as to seapower. The security of the battlewagons was, therefore, a major concern and both fleets had large numbers of cruisers and destroyers for the more economical exercise of regular duties. In 1914 the German fleet had twice as many destroyers as

Jellicoe had, and the latter thought his opponents might make fast raids on the Grand Fleet with these ships armed with torpedoes. The torpedo and the sea-mine were both relatively new weapons, and were serious threats to surface vessels. Decoy ships, old merchant vessels made up with wood and canvas to resemble dreadnoughts and nicknamed Jellicoe's Suicide Navy, constituted one attempt to protect the real battleships.

On 15 October 1914, one of Admiral de Chair's cruisers, HMS *Hawke*, was torpedoed about sixty miles east of Cromarty; she sank quickly and only seventy men from the 600-strong crew survived to be picked up later. De Chair moved his 10th Cruiser Squadron further north-west to patrol along a line from Shetland towards the north. The men on the line began to call themselves the Muckle Flugga Hussars, after the rock-bound northern tip of Shetland. Here it soon became clear that the ageing Edgar-class cruisers were not up to the task. A combination of bad weather, breakdowns, slow speed, and the frequent need to head for base to replenish coal stocks were endangering the effectiveness of the blockade. Modern mail steamers caused embarrassment by being faster than the intercepting cruisers. Some European skippers also resented being stopped by the Royal Navy and tried to outsmart the blockade. The Norwegians protested about interference with their shipping. Despite these tribulations, the cruisers stopped and searched many ships – on 14 October no fewer than fifty.

De Chair established his base in Swarbacks Minn, on the west side of mainland Shetland. This channel, roughly one mile wide, was guarded to north and south by the islands of Muckle Roe and Vementry, and led from Saint Magnus Bay into a deep sheltered anchorage in Busta Voe. The eighteenth-century mansion of Busta House was taken over as the shore headquarters; here the senior officers of the Northern Patrol indulged, in their off-duty hours, in some country-house living, while the ratings could find some recreation in a pub at Brae across the voe. In November, reports of U-boat activity led Jellicoe to order the evacuation of the Minn and despatch destroyers to scout for the enemy – nothing was found.

Strong gales in the same month finally brought an end to the vigil of the Edgar-class cruisers. The Squadron was ordered to the Clyde where seven of the ships were paid off and de Chair began to search for vessels that could stay at sea for prolonged periods in rough weather. The answer was to arm passenger liners. Almost half the world's merchant shipping in 1914 flew the Red Ensign and fortunately there was no shortage of vessels of the class required: 10,000 tons or more, and capable of speeds around 20 knots. Some were already under arms and one, the *Oceanic* of the White Star line, had come to grief on Foula on 8 September.

Fig. 8

The bridge and foredeck of the armed merchant cruiser Alsatian. *(author's collection)*

De Chair chose the Allan Line steamer *Alsatian*, also already commandeered, to be his flagship; before the War she had been carrying mail and passengers across the Atlantic and, cruising at 13.5 knots, she could stay at sea for forty-two days. Her top speed was 23 knots. The liners, known as armed merchant cruisers, or AMCs, had their decks strengthened and were armed with 6-inch and 4.7-inch guns; their cargo space was altered to make room for magazines and more coal. Eventually the 10th Squadron was to have twenty-five liners and eighteen armed trawlers, and a total complement of over 7,000 sailors. The men, who enjoyed some unusually spacious accommodation, were mixed companies of regular Royal Navy ratings and petty officers, some Royal Marines, and merchant seamen. Prominent among the latter were detachments from the Newfoundland naval reserve, like the men from the Hebrides and Shetland experts in handling small boats in rough seas.

Normally a liner's peace-time captain was given the rank of Commander RNR and remained as the master, with a Royal Navy officer in overall command, an arrangement that usually worked well but which was said by some to lie behind the fate of the *Oceanic*.[18] The merchant navy captain and the Royal Navy captain had disagreed over the course to follow and, cutting east of Foula in fog, the liner had strayed too near to the island with the result that she hit the reef called the Hivdi Grund. A homeward-bound Aberdeen trawler, the *Glenogil*, turned to assist the stricken liner. A cruiser, HMS *Forward*, then appeared from Lerwick but her attempt to tow off the *Oceanic* failed when the wire hawser parted. HMS *Hannibal* and the

Fig. 9

*Six-inch guns on
the* Alsatian.
(author's collection)

Alsatian also arrived on the scene. The *Glenogil* took off most of the 600
men aboard, leaving a small party aboard until around midnight, by which
time the wind had begun to rise and kick up a swell. By dawn the seas were
breaking over the *Oceanic* and it was clearly too late to save her – her back
broke and she became a total wreck.[19]

Despite some misgivings on the part of Admiral Jellicoe, Admiral de
Chair persevered in making Swarbacks Minn the base for the Northern
Patrol and by the summer of 1915 it was fully operational. This was how
Robert Manson from Westsandwick on the island of Yell found it when he
joined the RNR and was assigned to the staff in Busta House as personal
messenger to Rear-Admiral W.B. Fawckner, the commander of the shore
operation. The fifteen-year-old seaman – he had pretended to be older when
he had volunteered – was amazed by his first sight of the voe, bathed in
evening sunlight and filled with shipping of all shapes and sizes. Like many
Shetlanders, he knew the tragic story behind Busta House – how the
landlord, Gifford by name, had lost his three sons in a boating accident and
had died without a male heir – but this was the first time he had seen the
mansion, standing snugly among trees in its walled garden on the sheltered
north-west side of Busta Voe. The vessels anchored in the voe included the
Edgar-class cruiser HMS *Gibralter*, now assigned to less arduous duties as a
guard ship, sleek destroyers, freighters and colliers. A hospital ship, the
Berbice, was assigned to tend to the health needs of the Patrol. The Squadron
needed 1,600 tons of coal per day and a number of colliers were continually
keeping the base supplied. Robert Manson was to spend eighteen months as

Fawckner's messenger, a period he recorded as one of the happiest in his life.

Three trawlers patrolled the mouth of Swarbacks Minn in all weathers to challenge any approaching vessel. James Andrew Morrison served on one of the trawlers and recalled how, when westerly storms set in, all the little ships could do was heave to and ride them out: 'all we had to do was look out the window [of the wheelhouse] at the huge Atlantic waves with their white-crested tops coming marching on, in their never ceasing formation till they reached the high cliffs of Muckle Roe'.[20] When conditions grew too rough for comfort on a dark night, the trawler would sometimes move into a more sheltered spot until dawn. For a trawler to challenge the 10,000-ton liners of the Patrol involved some risk, as the big ships always came and went in the hours of darkness. They were frequently in a hurry to pass through the protecting boom and collisions occasionally resulted when the boom vessel failed to get out of the way in time.

For the crews of the AMCs out on patrol anywhere from the Hebrides to the Denmark Strait life was demanding. Once a cargo ship or a fishing boat had been intercepted and identified, a boarding party set off to row across to search the vessel – in calm weather perhaps not so difficult but in heavy seas a task requiring considerable seamanship, especially when the reception from the merchant skipper was less than cordial. A search of the intercepted ship was then carried out; any German nationals found aboard were arrested and, if the ship were judged to be carrying goods of value to the enemy, she was directed to head under armed guard to a British port for further examination. Lerwick and Kirkwall were the nearest harbours where this could be done. Every encounter between one of de Chair's ships and another vessel produced a unique situation. There was no telling what might happen or what might be found – a recalcitrant crew and an unco-operative master might be expected, but there was also the risk of collision or accident, of a U-boat appearing while the surface ships were not under way, or of the weather closing in. The boarding parties usually consisted of a handful of men led by a junior officer; they were armed but it still took some nerve for a young sub-lieutenant to impress his authority on a bluff Scandinavian skipper who until that moment may have been trying his hardest to outwit the Royal Navy and regarded his unwelcome guests as little better than pirates. Occasionally, though, a merchant skipper was grateful for the attentions of the Patrol: on 15 June 1915 a U-boat was preparing to sink the outward-bound Danish steamer *Russ* when the AMC *Orotava* hove into view, causing the German captain to break off his action and providing the *Russ* with a friendly escort.

Generally, the blockade was highly unpopular in the shipping circles of neutral countries. It interfered with the free commerce of the sea and drove

up costs. 'The government of Great Britain has virtually set up in the midst of the busy seas an arbitrary court, claiming unheard of powers and exercising the most tyrannous police functions', wrote a commentator in New York in 1915.[21] The seizing of cargoes meant that the ships of neutral countries began to refuse to carry goods for Germany. A few merchant captains, however, made a sport of pitting their wits against the Patrol and trying to evade detection: three ships of the Norske-Amerika Line – the *Bergensfjord*, the *Kristianiafjord* and the *Drammensfjord* – became notorious for their attempts, sometimes successful, to slip through the net. The Royal Navy compiled a blacklist of suspect neutrals. Various means were deployed by Germany herself to outwit the blockade and sometimes these found a measure of success, but within one year of the start of the War the blockade had begun drastically to affect daily life in central Europe. Food prices rose by as much as 65 per cent, and the cost of petrol doubled. By the end of July

Fig. 10

The armed merchant cruiser Orotava *entering Busta Voe.*
(author's collection)

Fig. 11

Ships of the Northern Patrol lying in Busta Voe.
(author's collection)

Fig. 12

One of the armed trawlers in the Northern Patrol. (author's collection)

1915, the Patrol had intercepted 1,610 ships, mostly vessels from Norway, Denmark, Sweden and USA, and had sent 396 into port for examination. Only one German ship, the *Rubens*, had been clever enough, or lucky enough, to evade the Patrol: on an outward passage, in February, she had sailed with supplies to the German forces in East Africa.

The freighters carrying iron ore from Narvik to Germany were able to bypass the blockade by sailing for most of their course very close to the Norwegian coast, often within Norway's jealously guarded territorial waters. The Patrol resorted to sending nimble armed trawlers inshore in an attempt to intercept them. On 30 June 1915, the trawler *Tenby Castle*, under the command of Lieutenant J.R. Randell RNR, identified a southbound freighter as the German-owned *Pallas* and fired a shot across her bows to command her to stop. *Pallas*'s captain stopped his engines but orientated his vessel so that her momentum might carry her into the safety of territorial waters in time. Randell spotted this plan and gave the captain five minutes to decide between following the trawler westward or being sent to the bottom. The German captain allowed the *Tenby Castle* boarding party to draw alongside but then rang for full speed ahead and made a break for it. Randell opened fire and hit the steering gear of the *Pallas*, causing her to wallow to a halt again. But this time she was safe: she was only two and a half miles offshore, well within neutral Norwegian waters, a situation made clear by the Norwegian patrol vessel that witnessed the incident and insisted on the *Pallas* being allowed to go on her way in accordance with international law. A few weeks later the British Foreign Office apologised to the Norwegian government for the *Tenby Castle*'s violation of her waters. Lieutenant

Fig. 13

*A boarding party lowering
away from the Alsatian)*

Fig. 14

*The boarding party
pulls to approach the
intercepted vessel.
(author's collection)*

Randell had some consolation a week later when the *Tenby Castle*
intercepted another German ore carrier, the *Friedrich Arp*; this time the interception was a safe distance outside territorial waters and, when the freighter
refused to follow him, Randell sank her.

The Northern Patrol never achieved the cutting of the iron-ore trade. A
proposal to send in a submarine to intercept the Narvik shipping was never
implemented. U-boats did come, however, in an attempt to locate blockade
ships and *U-22* torpedoed the AMC *India* off Vestfjord on 9 August 1915.
The *India* went down with the loss of 116 men, and the survivors were
interned by the Norwegian government in a camp at Lillehammer.

The Northern Patrol of the First World War was probably the last major
operation of its kind before the advent of aircraft altered the nature of sea
power. The exploits of the ships and men on the Patrol recall the days when
navies operated under sail. There were, in fact, still a considerable number of
sailing ships carrying freight in 1914 and, as the war progressed and shipping
costs rose, more were brought back into commission. The first neutral ship
the patrol sent into Lerwick for examination, in September 1914, was the

Norwegian sailing ship *Nordsie*. In July 1915 the AMC *Victorian* intercepted the American barque *Pass of Balmaha* bound for Archangel with a cargo of cotton, a particularly valuable commodity with military uses. The *Victorian's* boarding party of six men commanded her to sail to Kirkwall. Two days later, on 24 July, at seven o'clock in the morning, the enemy came alongside in the form of *U-36*. The men on the *Pass of Balmaha* had already seen *U-36* sink a trawler and two steamers, and now it looked like being their turn. The captain of *U-36*, however, decided not to sink the barque but send her, under his own men, to Germany. The men of the *Victorian* borrowed clothes from the American seamen and remained on-board undetected; they were desperate for an opportunity to retake the ship but the chance never came. The *Pass of Balmaha* somehow avoided other ships in the Northern Patrol and docked in Cuxhaven in August, where the cotton was welcomed and the *Victorian's* seamen became prisoners of war. Four days after the encounter with the barque, *U-36* fell victim to the Q-ship *Prince Charles* near North Rona, but the adventures of the *Pass of Balmaha* were not yet over, as we shall see.

John T. Hoseason was a prize crew officer on AMC *Ambrose* and on one

Fig. 15

In the First World War, there were still a considerable number of sailing vessels in the merchant trade. Here a boarding party approaches a barque. (author's collection)

Fig. 16

A 6-inch gun crew on the armed merchant cruiser Almanzora *in Arctic conditions.* (author's collection)

interception was given the task of bringing the Norwegian barque, *Lilian*, into Lerwick for examination. The *Lilian* was bound for home with a cargo of hogsheads of paraffin from New York, when the *Ambrose* stopped her far to the west of Orkney. Hoseason was instructed to chart a course around the north of Shetland to avoid the risk of meeting a U-boat in the Fair Isle Channel, and this he proceeded to do, a voyage that took the slow-moving barque almost four days. The Norwegian skipper was friendly and could vouch for all his crew except for two men who had joined them in New York. When the *Lilian* reached Lerwick, the two seamen revealed under interrogation that they really belonged to Hamburg and were arrested. Hoseason and his party returned to Busta Voe in two cars to await the arrival of the *Ambrose*.[22]

The most dramatic action between the liners of the Patrol and the enemy occurred on 29 February 1916. On that morning, in calm, overcast weather, the *Alcantara* and the *Andes* were dodging back and forth about 75 miles east of Unst, keeping a sharp look-out for an enemy raider they had been warned to expect. The two 15,000-ton ships, formerly of the Royal Mail Line, were relatively new – the *Alcantara* had been built in 1914 – and had been taken into armed service, with four others, in the spring of 1915. Captain T.E. Wardle RN was in command on the *Alcantara*. At nine o'clock the *Andes* spotted smoke to the north-east, and, almost at the same time, the *Alcantara*'s look-outs saw another plume to the west. The liners separated to investigate. At a range of 6,000 yards the *Alcantara* hoisted the flag signal commanding the strange ship to stop, and fired two blank rounds to reinforce the order. The stranger signalled compliance. With her crew at action stations and all her guns trained on the so-far unidentified ship, the *Alcantara* approached to within 4,000 yards. The *Andes*, meanwhile, was some 14 miles away, out of sight, pursuing the other vessel she had seen to the north-east. From the name and the flags painted on her hull Wardle saw that the strange ship was apparently the *Rena*, a Norwegian freighter homeward bound from Rio to Trondheim. Although there were still grounds for suspicion, the details seemed to fit and *Alcantara*'s boarding party prepared to launch. At this moment, the *Andes* steamed back into view and signalled by lamp 'That is suspicious vessel'.

Suddenly the *Rena* dropped the Norwegian ensign. A steering hut near the stern fell apart to reveal a 5.9-inch gun, and flaps for'ard of the bridge also dropped to uncover two more. The *Rena* opened fire at once. The boat the *Alcantara*'s boarding party was about to launch was shattered before it reached the water but the men, except for one fatality, were able to scramble back on board the liner. Another shell from the *Rena* hit the side of the *Alcantara*, wiping out her electrics and disabling the bridge steering controls. While Wardle and his men fought to activate the aft steering gear and the two vessels drifted closer to each other, the *Rena* kept up a fusillade of shells. *Alcantara*'s guns returned fire and set *Rena* ablaze in several places. The German ship – the *Rena* was in fact the raider *Greif* – then fired a torpedo that was observed to pass under the *Alcantara*'s stern. Some sources maintained the *Greif* fired a second torpedo but Captain Wardle said later that this was not the case. After about thirty minutes of desperate combat, the *Alcantara* was listing to starboard and taking on water. Some 800 yards away, the *Greif* was in worse shape and her crew began to abandon ship. Wardle ordered firing to cease. *Alcantara* settled and began to list to port. She was now beyond saving and, as her crew pulled away in their lifeboats and rafts, she sank.

The *Andes*, the cruiser HMS *Comus* and the destroyer HMS *Munster* at last arrived on the scene. The still burning *Greif* was finally committed to the deep by shellfire and the surviving crews of both ships were picked up: the *Alcantara* had lost two officers and sixty-seven men, the *Greif* around five officers and one hundred and twenty of her crew, including her captain, Fregatten-Kapitän Rudolf Tietze.

The naval activity in northern waters had a great impact on the towns in the islands. Kirkwall, nestling on the east side of its bay, was the older of Orkney's two towns, able to trace its origins back to the founding of Saint Magnus Cathedral by the Norse Earl Rognvald in the twelfth century. The population of Orkney was tremendously swollen, at times to over 100,000,

Fig. 17
*The San Francisco barque
Dirigo in Lerwick to have
her cargo examined for
contraband, 1916.
(Shetland Museum)*

by the presence of the Grand Fleet in Scapa Flow, and this had the inevitable consequences for local tradespeople and shopkeepers. Stromness on the west side of the Orkney Mainland was Kirkwall's rival as an urban centre; its sheltered haven had been welcoming ships since the beginnings of the Hudson's Bay Company in the 1600s, and it had grown with the swelling of North Atlantic trade and fisheries into a true sea town. The history of Lerwick, Shetland's county town, was somewhat similar to Stromness's. It too owed its birth on the west side of Bressay Sound to maritime activity, the annual arrival in Shetland of the Dutch herring fleet in the seventeenth century; and its growth had eclipsed the older settlement of Scalloway as the main centre of island life. Fort Charlotte, dominating the northern end of Lerwick, had been founded in 1665 and had been reconstructed during the American War of Independence, when it had been named after George III's queen. The towns were similar in that all three had a sinuous, narrow main street – aptly called Commercial Street in Lerwick's case – running through their hearts, and were the location for the main shops, markets, hotels and administrative buildings.

Captain Hubert G. Alston served as Senior Naval Officer (SNO) in Lerwick between March 1915 and January 1918. His predecessor had made his headquarters aboard a yacht but Alston established a shore base in three offices in the Fish Market, where his staff – a paymaster, three lieutenants, a warrant officer, a master-at-arms and a secretary – helped him run activities in the now busy harbour. The cruiser, HMS *Brilliant*, arrived in September 1915 to act as the base's parent ship: until her appearance, the base ship had been sited at Longhope, an unbelievably awkward bit of planning by the Admiralty in view of the way distance and the weather were bound to interrupt the fortnightly drifter assigned to bring up supplies. Lerwick was also the base for the Auxiliary Patrol, a group of steam yachts and other vessels armed to patrol local waters.

Kirkwall Bay and Bressay Sound became crowded with foreign ships sent in by the Northern Patrol for examination. Between July and September 1916, for example, 269 ships were searched by the Lerwick examining officers, and in 1917 more shipping tonnage passed through the Shetland port than any other harbour in Britain. The largest number of craft in the harbour at any one time happened on 23 September 1917 when 139 vessels lay at anchor. To cope with the demand, Captain Alston set up an examination office staffed by two officers and four interpreters. Examining cargoes remained, however, a tricky business as it was impossible in a reasonable time to search all the potential hiding places aboard a steamer. As it was, a considerable quantity of contraband goods was seized. Over 100

German sailors were also caught trying to reach home aboard neutral ships. Alston recalled one incident:

> a ship was under examination whose cargo was onions. The Examination Officer was rather suspicious as he was not aware that onions were exported from the port she was from. He could find nothing wrong, however, and was on the verge of passing the cargo when an onion he was holding slipped to the deck, and, to his surprise, it bounced. Immediately he got hold of it again, started to get the skin off, and found inside a nice ball of rubber.[23]

The towns also became the centres of major supply and ancillary operations, a development that brought attendant dangers: an Admiralty store filled with TNT exploded on the Alexandria Wharf at Lerwick on 12 April 1915 killing seven people and wounding many more. Lena Mouat had just started as the SNO's secretary when it happened: 'I was standing in a corner beside the window [of the office] when there was a terrific bang,' she wrote, 'and instantly the office became a shambles with the glass flying in with such force that it stuck in the opposite wall, and every piece of furniture turning over.'[24] On another occasion, four men were killed when a depth charge exploded on the trawler *Tenby Castle*.

A wide range of look-out posts, signal stations and defence installations sprang up throughout the islands. A radio station at Voxter in the district of Cunningsburgh listened in to U-boat transmissions. Gun batteries guarded the approaches to Kirkwall Bay, Scapa Flow, Bressay Sound and Swarbacks Minn. The mounting of guns on Bard Head and Aith Head to cover the approaches to Lerwick involved hoisting them from lighters up the 300-foot cliffs on sheers; the boilers operating the winches had to be anchored to the ground to stop gales blowing them away. The Orkney batteries were manned by the local Territorial Force of the Royal Garrison Artillery, with additional Royal Marine and Navy personnel in not always happy combination. Royal Marines garrisoned the guns in Shetland, while the guarding of the strategically important cable stations was made the responsibility first of territorial forces and later of retired RNR personnel. Other gun crews were later placed in some of the outlying parts of the islands, and telephone and wireless communication networks were set up. The foundations of many of the installations remain to this day.

Not all the gun crews were perhaps as efficient as their situation warranted. Rear-Admiral Fawckner had some mobile gun crews based at strategic points to respond to sightings of U-boats inshore. A former Indian

Fig. 18
The members of the Women's Royal Naval Service (WRNS) at the naval base in Lerwick, probably taken in 1918. (Shetland Museum)

Army officer commanded such a crew in Yell. One morning the crew was called out to deal with a U-boat spotted in Whalefirth Voe. The crew raced to the scene in their army truck, towing a six-pounder gun, only to discover when they reached their destination that they had neglected to bring the ammunition.

The civilian sections of the population also played their part in the war effort by raising funds, laying on entertainments and hospitality for the visitors, knitting items of clothing for the serving troops, and generally taking part in such activities as collecting and drying sphagnum moss for surgical dressings. A day in July 1917 was set aside as a holiday so that everyone could go to the moors to collect sphagnum. The Church Army provided a recreation hut in response to a request from Captain Alston; it was erected and run by the people of Lerwick, and provided a welcome haven for seamen ashore, and served food, clothing and first aid to the survivors brought to the town from torpedoed ships.

While the Northern Patrol enforced the strategy of blockading of commercial shipping, the Grand Fleet, in its bases at Scapa Flow, Invergordon and Rosyth, remained poised to meet the threat of the German High Seas Fleet. The single major confrontation between them happened over the evening and night of 31 May–1 June 1916 in the well-documented Battle of Jutland, the biggest seafight in history between armed fleets, in which a total of some 250 ships, ranging in size from battleships down to destroyers, tried to outguess and outgun each other. The result in retrospect was a draw – both fleets emerged from the smoke and darkness with their potential largely intact – but at the time the clash turned into a strategic victory for the Royal Navy. After Jutland the major part of the High Seas Fleet remained at anchor until it surrendered to the Allies in 1918. Germany fell back on two weapons to continue the war at sea and attempt to combat the stranglehold of the blockade – the U-boat and the surface raider. With the former she almost succeeded.

The sea war in the north-east Atlantic developed into a contest in the disruption of trade. U-boats and open-ocean raiders set out from Germany to sneak through the watching British screen and strike at merchant shipping, as the blockading ships of the Royal Navy similarly strove to prevent vessels from carrying supplies to the continental power.

The early types of submarine were unable to stay submerged for long periods and underwater the speed was slow – only some 8 knots. The first U-boats in the German fleet were powered by paraffin engines but by the start of the War diesel engines had been introduced, and the latest craft had enough range to reach the west coast of Britain and return. These U-boats were armed with four torpedo tubes and a deck gun for surface action. Germany had twenty ready for sea in August 1914, with a further eight under repair or otherwise non-operational. The Royal Navy had seventy-four, almost three times as many, but did not consider them to have much to offer in an offensive role, thinking them better suited for fleet defence and reconnaissance. To many officers of the old school, sneaking up on the enemy in a submarine was an ungentlemanly thing to do. Germany was to build many more U-boats, with developments in design and performance, in the following four years – the fleet totalled 344 by the end of the War, and another 200 were on the stocks – and the attacks on shipping were to increase to a critically disruptive level for Britain's war effort.

In January 1914, Lord Fisher, then acting as an unofficial adviser to Churchill, had written a long memorandum on how the submarine would upset everything. The submarine menace, said Fisher, was 'a truly terrible one' and its existence had undermined the traditional strategy of blockade and meant Britain had to fear, not invasion, but starvation.[25] He was repeating, albeit in more dramatic terms, a warning made by Admiral Sir A.K. Wilson in 1910 that the major threat the country faced was directed at the merchant fleet and the disruption of trade.

Not everyone shared Lord Fisher's view and both sides took a little time to realise the potential of this new type of warship. Two days after the outbreak of the war, ten U-boats set off towards Scapa Flow with the main aim of establishing where the British were setting up their blockade line. This mission was unsuccessful and two U-boats were lost: one of them, *U-15*, was forced by engine trouble to surface where she was spotted and rammed by HMS *Birmingham*. The fear of U-boat attack led, however, to false 'periscope alarms' in Scapa Flow. On 23 November *U-18* did manage almost to penetrate the Grand Fleet's defences, but was detected and sunk after a dramatic chase in the Pentland Firth. The first British warship to succumb to a U-boat attack was HMS *Pathfinder*, off St Abb's Head on 5 September 1914. This sinking was soon followed by the same fate being meted swiftly out to three elderly cruisers – HMS *Aboukir*, HMS *Cressy* and HMS *Hogue* – on patrol off the Dutch coast on 22 September.

The German command immediately began to consider the U-boats as a way to counter the British blockade and impose one of their own on the enemy's merchant shipping. The first British merchant ship, indeed the first merchant ship of any nation, to fall victim to a submarine was the relatively small, 866-ton coaster *Glitra*. Off the south Norwegian coast on 20 October, *U-17* fired a shot across the bows of the *Glitra* to stop her. The German boarding party ordered the crew to take to their boats and opened the sea cocks on the freighter to sink her. The captain of *U-17* then did the gentlemanly thing of towing the *Glitra*'s crew in their boats until they were safely in Norwegian waters.

The U-boat fleet sank some 20,000 tons of British shipping (ten ships) in the first five months of the war, a mere foretaste of what was to come. At this time the German navy operated according to the internationally recognised Prize Rules, sinking a ship only after the crew had been given a warning and time to escape. Two U-boats applied these rules in an attack on a fleet of herring drifters north-east of Shetland on 23 June 1915. Some of the twenty steam drifters cut their nets loose when they saw the enemy and tried to make a run for the coast but did not escape. In six hours the Germans methodically sank sixteen of the fishing boats, allowing the crew of each one to transfer to one of the four drifters they had chosen as rescue boats. The U-boats towed the small boats to speed up the transfers. Two of the drifter crews made it on their own to the Out Skerries, one of them having had a helpful tow for a few miles from one of their attackers. The news of this striking event reached Lerwick on the following day when the four spared drifters – *Nigella*, *A.M. Leask*, *Energy* and *Archimedes* – steamed into port.[26]

Captain Alston implemented a scheme to snare U-boats in fishing nets: he had his men lay or tow some 40-50 miles of driftnet in Shetland waters but this primitive countermeasure failed to catch a submarine, although there were a few false alarms. The nets were fitted with calcium floats that lit up when the net was struck; one warning went off on a net in the Fair Isle Channel but, according to Captain Alston, 'after some hours of intense excitement the catch turned out to be a whale ... This sort of thing happened once or twice and I believe some of the drifters' crews are convinced to this day that some of the catches were submarines.'

A salvage department to deal with damaged shipping was set up in Lerwick. Some of the freighters, after being hit by a torpedo or a mine, only stayed afloat because they happened to be carrying a cargo of timber from Norway. An incidental consequence of this aspect of the war was a richer harvest for northern beachcombers. Captain Alston noted that at one time no fewer than seven ships lay on the bottom of Lerwick harbour; all of them were later raised successfully.

Older naval officers regarded sea mines as much as submarines as awful weapons, but both sides deployed them in the War in large numbers. Any ship at any time might encounter one of these floating bombs, ready to explode on contact, and, as the War progressed, dealing with them, essentially

Fig. 19

HMS Rosabelle *recovering
a Type 2 German mine.
(Orkney Library)*

minesweeping, became a dangerous but necessary activity. On the first night
of the War the minelayer *Königin Luise* sped across the North Sea to lay
mines off the Suffolk coast. This bold move ended in disaster when the cruiser
HMS *Amphion* spotted the minelayer and sank her, but on the following day
the effectiveness of the sea mine was demonstrated when the victorious
Amphion struck one of the *Königin Luise*'s mines herself and was lost.

The technology was similar on both sides. The British mine, laid in
extensive fields in various parts of the North Sea, consisted of a sphere of
explosive designed to float some 5-10 feet under the surface of the sea at high
water. They were held in place by a mooring cable attached to an anchoring
weight on the seabed and exploded on direct contact with a ship's hull. U-boat
skippers learned to negotiate these minefields by dodging through them at or
near the surface at low water, or by going deep to weave through the mooring
cables. The deployment of anti-submarine nets was more effective as a U-boat
deterrent in confined waters – attempts to use them around Shetland have
been noted above – and their use off the south-east English coast led to U-
boats always preferring the northabout route to the Atlantic. Further
problems were caused by mines that broke loose from their moorings to drift
inshore or wherever tide and currents would carry them.

On 27 October 1914, the dreadnought HMS *Audacious* succumbed to a
German mine off the coast of Ireland, but the most famous victim of this
weapon is probably the cruiser HMS *Hampshire*. On the evening of 5 June

1916, en route to Russia in a fierce north-westerly gale with Lord Kitchener aboard, she struck a mine off the west coast of the Orkney Mainland and sank with a heavy loss of life. *U-80* sowed mines across the entrance to Swarbacks Minn on 7 March 1917 and disrupted the movements of the Northern Patrol until it could be swept by trawlers. One mine at least escaped detection and a week after the *U-80*'s clandestine visit the AMC *Motagua* struck it, but was able to struggle into Swarbacks Minn.

The approaches to Lerwick were mined in January 1917 by a U-boat, a practice the Germans often repeated thereafter. The destroyer *Bullfinch* hit one of them and, as Captain Alston had no sweepers, he declared the harbour closed; sweepers from the Grand Fleet came up from Scapa Flow and found seven mines. The naval authorities in Lerwick instituted their own mine patrol with trawlers. It was probably inevitable that, although two channels were swept every day, some mines would be missed or a minelaying U-boat might creep in quickly to replace what the sweepers' paravanes had released. On 30 June 1917 the destroyer HMS *Cheerful* struck a mine two miles east of Aithsetter and went down with the loss of forty-one hands. In September two leading ships in an outward bound convoy were mined and sunk; when the minesweepers searched the area for a second time they detected six mines where there had been none an hour before. Captain Alston wrote:

We were able to get a little satisfaction for this deed shortly afterwards, as we managed to sink *UG 55*, a submarine minelayer. Apparently, something had gone wrong with her internally and she came to the surface outside the harbour. A destroyer and some trawlers near, immediately attacked her and she very soon was sunk, eight of the crew being rescued and brought in. She had not laid her mines, and the destroyer went across to her and dropped a depth charge which caused a frightful explosion.[23]

The Lerwick base had a few tense moments on another occasion when one of the armed trawlers in the Auxiliary Patrol came into harbour with a captured German mine secured under her stern. The mine was towed back out to sea to be sunk. This kind of deed was typical of the hardy RNR officers and fishermen who crewed the patrol.

The German campaign against British shipping also involved the deployment of sea raiders, equivalent to the liners adapted to serve on the Northern Patrol in that they were ships originally built for peaceful purposes but converted as armed war vessels. They had to evade the Northern Patrol

Fig. 20
A mine ashore at Virkie.
(Shetland Museum)

to reach the Atlantic, and the fate of one that failed to make it, the *Greif,* has already been described. The most famous to escape the keen eyes of the Patrol was the *Möwe* (Gull), under Count Nikolaus zu Dohna-Schlodien. The *Möwe* slipped north along the Norwegian coast in December 1915 and entered the Atlantic from the Arctic. After sowing some mines in the waters around Sule Skerry, one of which claimed HMS *Edward VII* on 6 January 1916, she sank fifteen Allied or neutral ships before cleverly dodging the Northern Patrol again to win home to Wilhelmshaven on 4 March. Between November 1916 and March 1917, the *Möwe* undertook a second foray into the Atlantic, this time boldly cutting through the Shetland–Faroe gap at night, and again returned safely to her home port, having accounted for a further six merchant ships.

The American sailing ship *Pass of Balmaha*, whose capture has already been described, was converted into a raider and despatched again to sea in December 1916 from Bremen with a new name – *Seeadler* (Sea eagle). Under her captain, Count Felix von Luckner, she disguised herself so successfully as a Norwegian ship that the boarding party from the AMC *Avenger*, when she was stopped and searched south-west of Iceland, were completely fooled. The *Seeadler* went on her way and sank ten ships before coming to grief by being wrecked in Fiji in August 1917.

With the High Seas Fleet swinging on its anchor chains in home waters, the U-boat remained the main offensive weapon in the arsenal of the German navy. Several encounters took place in the waters around Orkney and Shetland. The armed yachts *Duke of Albany* and *Duke of Clarence* sailed from Longhope on the morning of 24 August 1916 and were zigzagging past the Pentland Skerries at 0900 hours when the officer of the watch on the *Duke of Albany*, Lieutenant Norman Leslie RNR, spotted a torpedo track on the port beam. Leslie immediately ordered a change of course and rang the gong for action stations but his attempt to avoid the weapon flashing towards the ship failed. The torpedo – Leslie saw it clearly on the surface and described it later as brilliant red with a black head – struck the *Duke of Albany* amidships, blasting a column of water and a lifeboat into the air. At that moment Leslie saw another torpedo pass astern. Half a mile away to starboard the *Duke of Clarence* dropped lifeboats for the benefit of her companion's crew and began to circle at full speed in an attempt to locate or drive off their attacker. An object was seen under the surface about half a mile ahead and the *Duke of Clarence* fired on it before steering directly over the supposed location in the hope of ramming the U-boat; however, nothing was struck or felt. Twenty-five men went down with the *Duke of Albany*, including her captain, Commander George Ramage RNR.[28]

On the afternoon of 26 September 1916 the armed yacht *Conqueror II* and the armed trawler *Sarah Alice* were patrolling between Sumburgh Head and Fair Isle. At half past four, about 12 miles north by west of North Point, she intercepted the Glasgow steamer *St Gothard*, en route from Swarbacks Minn to the Firth of Forth, to check her identity. Just as the *St Gothard* was setting off again, a torpedo streaked past her bow and struck the *Sarah Alice*. The hapless trawler sank at once with the loss of all hands. As the crew of the *Conqueror II* rushed to action stations and prepared to fire at the periscope now visible some 300 yards on the starboard bow, a second torpedo hit her. The yacht broke in half and sank in three minutes. Alexander Laing, the skipper of the *St Gothard,* ordered a boat away to rescue survivors from the other two ships but then realised from the position of the periscope that his vessel was the next target and decided it was time to abandon ship.

The mainly Greek crew of the *St Gothard* pulled away in their two lifeboats and watched the expected torpedo burst against the hull of their ship, sending a pillar of water 500 feet into the air. The spray fell on the seamen, drenching them at their oars. With a rush of steam and the rumble of an internal explosion, the *St Gothard* slid stern first beneath the choppy sea. Now the waves parted and the grey hull of the U-boat appeared. Laing was ordered by the Germans to come alongside and surrender his ship's papers. He answered that they had gone down with the ship and was then told to pull eastward where a trawler would pick them up. Laing and his men found that they could make little headway rowing into the east wind and instead shaped their course northward, eventually reaching safety at Walls the following morning.

The other lifeboat from the *St Gothard*, under the command of the mate, Daniel McIntosh, became separated from its companion. The U-boat had meanwhile fished two men from the *Conqueror II* from the sea and now the German captain handed them over to McIntosh's care before firing signal rockets in the hope of attracting help for the seamen. McIntosh and his colleagues were picked up by the destroyer HMS *Sylvia* from Lerwick at half past midnight. One of the two men rescued by the U-boat, Lieutenant Thomas Davis RNR, had been badly wounded in the action and died aboard the destroyer, but sixteen of the *Conqueror II's* total complement of thirty-seven were eventually rescued. Neither McIntosh nor any of his companions was able to identify the U-boat beyond thinking it was of the UC or UB type.[29]

Two ships of the North of Scotland, Orkney and Shetland Shipping Company, the main carrier of passengers and freight between the islands and the Scottish mainland, and universally known as the North boats, also fell victim to submarines. The *St Margaret* was torpedoed on 12 September 1917 when she was 30 miles east of the Faroes en route to Iceland. Five of the crew went down with her but her captain, William Leask, and the rest of his men sailed for three days in their lifeboat to reach safety at Hillswick on the Shetland Mainland. A few months later, on 19 January 1918, Captain Leask was in command of the *St Clair* when she was threatened by a U-boat off Fair Isle but on this occasion he managed to drive off the enemy and was awarded the DSC. The *St Magnus* became the second North boat to be torpedoed, off Peterhead on 12 February 1918.[30]

The chivalrous conduct embodied in the Prize Rules was to be abandoned as the War dragged on and the contest between the belligerents grew more intense. Disputes broke out several times in the German high command over the declaration of unrestricted warfare at sea, as the growing realisation of the efficacy of the submarine ran up against the need to maintain diplomatic relations with neutral nations, especially the USA. On 4 February 1915 Germany announced that the waters around Britain were to be considered a war zone where Allied shipping could be sunk without warning but this policy was reversed in the following September when the sinking of the *Lusitania* raised a storm of international protest. U-boats again began to operate in British waters in February 1916 and in October of that year reverted once more to observing Prize Rules. The final and fatal reversal of policy took place on 1 February 1917, the date on which U-boats were ordered to launch unrestricted warfare on all shipping in European waters.

The continual interception of commercial shipping by the Northern Patrol was having a disastrous effect on the German economy, causing severe shortages of food, fodder and other goods during the winter of 1916–17. By this time, the British government had formed agreements with many neutral nations and shipowners to strengthen the efficiency of the blockade. In May 1915 the Norske-Amerika Line agreed to supply information on their cargoes. Neutral ships began to be examined in port before they set sail and several large harbours, Halifax, Kingston, Port Said and Freetown among them, became centres for examination. In March 1916 the so-called Navicert system was introduced to certify the contents of cargoes in ships bound from America to Scandinavia – those with a Navicert were allowed to steam through the Patrol without hindrance. The consequence of this system was that the Royal Navy could now regard any unexamined vessel as of value to the enemy and seize it. The British government also took the unusual step of buying most of Norwegian fish landings to prevent re-export to Germany. So effective were these various measures that Germany's imports had virtually dried up by the beginning of 1917, the only commodity still getting through in reasonable quantities being iron ore from northern Scandinavia.

However, there was a lighter side to this grim reality, as Robert Manson found out in a dockside café in Hamburg in 1921. By then, like many of his fellow Shetlanders, Robert had joined the merchant service and was trading into Germany on a Currie Line freighter. He befriended the café owner, an ex-U-boat commander who, as it happened, had operated mainly in the area north and west of Shetland. When Robert told him that he came from Shetland, the former adversary grew excited and asked if Robert knew the area of Whalefirth Voe, a four-mile-long inlet on the west side of Yell.

'When I told him that I lived only three mile from the Voe, the café owner grasped me by the hand … German submarines, he said, were poorly supplied with food and on long patrols fresh meat generally ran out very quickly. Early in the War, he had found that Whalefirth Voe offered ideal conditions for lying on the bottom and he used to go there from time to time for a rest – keeping watch through his periscope on the work of the place. After a few visits, it became apparent that sheep frequented the shore to eat seaweed when the tide was out. One night the Germans launched their dinghy, paddled into a geo and soon had captured two animals which they carried aboard, slaughtered and enjoyed. This practice went on until Whalefirth Voe became their standard source of fresh meat. One dark night they landed near to the village and found a large animal with horns conveniently tethered. It was soon on board the dinghy and on its way to the pot. However, that meat tasted bitter and made them sick – but that was the only bad meat that they came across in Whalefirth Voe.[31]

Robert was able to tell the former submariner that the disappearance of this particular sheep – a prize ram belonging to a crofter called Andrew Mann – was well remembered and had been the subject of great speculation at the time. Who on earth, the crofters had asked, would want to steal a ram at the height of the tupping season, when the beast was dangerous and its flesh would in any case be raunchy and inedible?

Germany declared unrestricted submarine warfare in February 1917 partly in an attempt to break the stranglehold on her overseas trade. Ships of the Northern Patrol were among the victims at this time: the *Hilary* was torpedoed on 25 May and the *Avenger* on 14 June while she was steaming towards Scapa Flow. Two more of the AMCs fell to the enemy later that year: the *Otway* on 22 July and the *Champagne* on 9 October.

In March 1916, Admiral de Chair was appointed to a post in the Admiralty and his position at Swarbacks Minn was filled by Admiral Sir Reginald Tupper, known as Holy Reggie in the Navy through his fondness for church services. Tupper happened to be the brother-in-law of Rear-Admiral Fawckner who was in charge of the Patrol's shore operation based at Busta House.

By the end of 1915, U-boats had sunk 855,000 tons of Allied shipping, almost ninety per cent of this total being British. In return, only twenty U-boats had been lost. After another year the number of British ships sunk had reached an amount equivalent to one fifth of her merchant fleet and losses continued to rise dramatically after the declaration of unrestricted warfare. The record loss was reached in April 1917 when 881,000 tons of Allied commercial shipping, three quarters of it British, went to the bottom. At this rate Britain was losing a tenth of her fleet every month. Lord Jellicoe, by this time First Sea Lord, told Rear-Admiral William Sims of the United States Navy that in this period the U-boats almost achieved victory and if the loss of ships had continued at the rate reached in early 1917 Britain would have found it impossible to continue. In fact the Allies were losing vessels faster than they could be replaced and it was calculated that no more than six weeks would see the end.

Tactics such as the deployment of Q ships – armed vessels sailing disguised as harmless merchantmen to lure U-boats into an ambush – had scored a few successes but the U-boat captains soon grew wary of seemingly innocent tramp ships and resorted more and more to attacking while submerged. Fifteen out of the sixteen Q ships listed in the 1919 edition of *Jane's Fighting Ships of World War I* were themselves torpedoed, and the sixteenth foundered after being torpedoed. One of the trawlers of the Auxiliary Patrol based at Lerwick, the *Sitvel*, was fitted out as a Q-ship, her guns disguised or hidden, but she failed to entrap any U-boats.

The depth charge made its appearance in January 1916 and proved to be the most effective weapon against submarines but there was no way of detecting craft underwater and aerial reconnaissance was still in its infancy. What tipped the scales in favour of an Allied victory was the introduction of convoys and the entry into the war of the USA on 6 April 1917, itself a development stemming directly from the U-boat offensive. It took a long time for the Admiralty to overcome strong prejudices among its officer corps and decide to introduce convoys on some trade routes. What the supporters of convoy had argued all along became apparent very soon – ships were far safer from U-boat attack sailing in escorted groups. The rate of destruction

Fig. 21

*A convoy passes Copinsay
on the east coast of
Orkney in 1918.
(Copyright IWM.
No. Q 102252)*

dropped dramatically: only five ships were lost out of 800 in convoys in July
and August. U-boats found fewer and fewer merchant craft sailing alone and
were forced to approach a convoy in search of a target, a manoeuvre that put
them also at increased risk of attack. The German navy did not change its
tactics to respond to this development and, in September 1917, ten U-boats
were destroyed, the first time the rate of loss exceeded the rate of
construction.

The enterprising Captain Alston at Lerwick instituted the convoy
principle on his own initiative in the autumn of 1916 by providing escorts
from among his patrolling ships for some merchantmen passing between
Shetland and Norway, but it was not until the following April that convoys
officially began on this relatively short passage. These became the target of
sorties by German surface ships towards the end of 1917. The western
assembly point for the Norwegian convoys was a few miles to the south of
Lerwick. On 17 October a convoy of twelve merchant ships was 65 miles
east of Shetland, inward bound from Bergen, when it was attacked by two
cruisers, the *Bremse* and the *Brummer*. The escorting destroyers, *Mary Rose*
and *Strongbow*, did what they could against the superior enemy but they and

nine of the convoy were sunk. One of the trawler escorts, the *Elise*, managed to pick up some survivors and bring them to Lerwick.

In December another raid, this time by four destroyers, accounted for an entire eastward-bound convoy. This group, comprising six colliers with an escort of two destroyers, the *Pellew* and the *Partridge*, and four armed trawlers, left Lerwick late on the morning of the 11th. Twenty-four hours later the convoy was some 30 miles from the Norwegian coast, making steady progress at 7 knots. At 11.30 a.m. the *Pellew* and the *Partridge* sighted warships to the north-west. When the challenge to the approaching strangers was wrongly answered, the destroyers realised they were in the presence of the enemy and sped ahead to intercept while the convoy and its close trawler escort began to scatter. The German force, the 3rd Half-Flotilla under the command of Hans Kolbe, comprising the four destroyers *V100*, *V32*, *G101* and *G102*, began a two-pronged attack. While three of Kolbe's ships engaged the two British destroyers, the fourth proceeded to attack the convoy. The *Partridge* was so badly hit by the accurate, rapid enemy gunfire that her captain ordered her to be abandoned; the *Pellew*, hit in the engine room and crippled, escaped when a providential squall of rain swept over her and hid her from view. She was later able to limp towards the Norwegian coast and safety.

Meanwhile the fourth attacker picked off the convoy ships one by one. All six freighters, five of which belonged to neutral Scandinavian countries, and the four escorting trawlers – the *Lord Alverstone*, *Livingstone*, *Tokio* and *Commander Fullerton* – were sunk. The crew of the *Lord Alverstone* abandoned ship and, after rowing all night, reached the Norwegian fishing village of Hevrø; here they were looked after by the villagers until they were collected by a Norwegian gunboat and brought to Bergen, before going on to internment at Jörstadmoen near Lillehammer.

The wireless signals flashed from the *Partridge* as the fight began were jammed by the German ships and no contact could be made with Lerwick. However, a message from the *Pellew* was picked up by a British squadron, led by the cruiser HMS *Shannon*, some miles to the south. Although too far away to be able to reach the scene of the action in time, they were able to rescue some survivors. The Admiralty Court of Enquiry concluded that it had been a mistake to have the east-bound and the west-bound convoys at sea at the same time, with the covering force unable to protect both.[32] Convoys were provided with increased protection after this incident to the extent that Admiral Reinhard Scheer, commanding the High Seas Fleet, considered making a large raid against them in the hope of drawing the Grand Fleet once again into battle. One attempt to realise this ambition was made in

Fig. 22
An artist's impression of the armed trawler Lord Alverstone. *(author)*

Fig. 23
HMS Partridge *at speed.*
(Copyright IWM.
No. SP 902)

H.M.S. LORD ALVERSTONE.
SUNK. Dec. 1st. 1917.

April 1918 but it came to naught when the German fleet failed to find a convoy.

The gathering of merchant shipping into convoys and the subsequent fall in the number of ships sailing on their own led to less and less for the Northern Patrol to do. Some of the armed liners were withdrawn to serve as convoy escorts and at the end of November 1917 the Patrol was officially disbanded. In the thirty-nine months of its existence the Patrol had intercepted some 13,000 vessels; 1,816 had been sent into port for examination and only a few hundred had managed to evade interception. Some 7,000 officers and men had served in the patrol and, considering all causes from bad weather to enemy action, the service had lost 10 ships and 2 trawlers, and a total of 1,166 hands.

The base in Swarbacks Minn was closed and a new headquarters for all naval activities in Shetland was established in Brentham House in Harbour Street, Lerwick, called HMS *Ambitious*. Rear-Admiral Clement Greatorex, who had commanded the Northern Patrol in its last two months, was now the SNO; Captain Alston's post was renamed Captain of the Base.

The United States declared war on Germany on 6 April 1917 and in the last month of the year, on 7 December, Battleship Division 9 of the US Navy, led by Rear Admiral Hugh Rodman flying his flag on USS *New York*, arrived in Scapa Flow. Thereafter the American ships, designated the 6th Battle Squadron of the Grand Fleet, shared patrol, blockade and escort duties with the Royal Navy. Meanwhile the assaults by U-boats on Allied shipping continued. Although losses fell after the introduction of the convoy system – from 685,000 tons in June 1917 to an average of 140,000 tons per month in June to October 1918 – the lean, underwater attackers remained a major threat. The US Navy came up with the idea of reinforcing the blockade of the North Sea by laying a barrage of mines across the Orkney–Norway gap to supplement the extensive minefields in the Channel and the Heligoland Bight, creating a barrier through which, it was hoped, the U-boats would be unable to penetrate. The Admiralty had considered extensive mine barrages earlier in the War but had laid the idea aside as being too costly and difficult. Their lordships required some convincing that this was now a sensible thing to do, objecting, for example, that the immense minefield would interfere with the free movement of the Grand Fleet, but the Americans' persistence won the day and the mine-laying operation began.

Towards the end of June 1918, the minelayers or, in American parlance, mineplanters arrived at their bases in Invergordon and Inverness, where the tender and flagship *Black Hawk* was stationed, and over the next few months laid thousands of mines, sometimes in difficult, stormy conditions. In her 3-month stint, the *Aroostook*, like most of the mineplanters a converted passenger ship, steamed over 4,000 miles and planted 2,510 mines. The *Saranac* had planted almost 5,000 by the end of October. Eventually the Americans had spread a forest of over 56,000 mines over the central sector of the Barrage, and the British an additional 16,000 in their sectors adjacent to Orkney and the Norwegian coast.[33]

The extent of the barrage was announced in newspapers, for example in the *Orkney Herald* on 15 May 1918. According to this, it took the form of a triangle with its apex in the Arctic and its southern boundary stretching from Norway to the Butt of Lewis, touching the north-east of Caithness; it included all Orkney and Shetland, and totalled 121,782 square miles. All shipping, ordered the Admiralty, was to keep out of the area 'from half an hour after sunset to half an hour before sunrise unless at anchor'. Only naval vessels were allowed to move at night, and stringent regulations were applied to the approaches to Kirkwall and Scapa Flow. Neutral ships were forbidden to traffic to Shetland, and the Pentland Firth was made off limits altogether. In fact, this announcement contained some disinformation, for the barrage varied between 15 and 35 miles in width, formidable enough. The barrage was hardly complete before rumours began to circulate that the War was drawing to a close. In a final desperate attack, *U-116* tried to sneak into Scapa Flow through Hoxa Sound but was detected by hydrophones linked to mines and blown up with all hands. It is unknown how many U-boats were caught in the barrage itself – estimates vary between six and ten either destroyed or damaged, not a high number in view of the intense effort put into the laying of the mines – but the supporters of the scheme pointed out that the War ended before its value could really be tested. Until the very last months of the War, U-boats could still slip around the eastern, unmined end in Norwegian territorial waters.

The announcement of the Armistice on 11 November was marked by jubilation in the northern islands and the units stationed there, as it was in the rest of the country. A wireless message brought the good news to Scapa Flow and the naval vessels began to sound their sirens, alerting the islanders to what had happened. Church bells began to peal, people crowded into the street in Kirkwall, and at noon the town crier proclaimed a half-holiday.[34] Some wartime restrictions continued in force for almost a year but were gradually eased as the months went by and armistice turned into peace. By this time the people were impatient to return to their normal peacetime routines and were counting the costs of the War.

In human terms, the casualty figures had cut a swathe through a

Fig. 24

The German High Seas
Fleet interned in Scapa
Flow in November 1918.
(Copyright IWM.
No. HU 90006)

generation. For example, nearly 60 per cent, over 4,200 men, of the male population of Shetland between the ages of 15 and 64 had served their country, mainly in the Royal Navy and the Reserve although also in the merchant marine and the Army [35] some 600 did not come home. The effect of the war was seen most strongly in the communities on some of the smaller islands: half of the men between 18 and 40, 32 in number, left the small Orkney island of North Ronaldsay and only 15 returned to live there.[36]

Orkney's population had been boosted for the four years by the complements of the Grand Fleet, some 100,000 men. Shetland had had to host fewer numbers but, in both archipelagos, more land was brought into cultivation. Despite the shortages of labour and horses, yields of grain, vegetables and livestock rose in response to better prices and the need to feed all the incomers. Increased profits allowed many Orkney farmers to buy their holdings in the years after the War. Naval activity, restrictions on navigation and the loss of manpower to the armed forces disrupted the fishing but, despite these handicaps, valuable catches of herring and white fish continued to be landed. There was a high demand for Shetland knitwear. All in all the War, in economic terms, was a boom time and people saved against harder days ahead: deposits in the Commercial Bank in Lerwick doubled between 1913 and 1919.

In November 1918 the German High Seas Fleet was interned in Scapa Flow. The ships, with much reduced crews, lay there over the winter while the post-War peace negotiations dragged on in France. At last, in midsummer 1919, the German commander implemented an extraordinary and successful act of sabotage in which the whole Fleet scuttled to avoid an ignominious surrender. This episode has been described in detail elsewhere, along with the major salvage operation to raise many of the sunk ships in the inter-war years.[37]

The minefields laid during the War were now a major hazard to shipping and an elaborate sweeping operation was put into action to retrieve them or blow them up in situ. The main base for the removal of the North Sea Barrage was established in Kirkwall and, as with the laying of the mines, ships of the United States Navy played a prominent part alongside the trawlers and tenders of the Royal Navy. The *Black Hawk*, under Commander R.C. Bulmer, moved north from Inverness to act as the flagship for the minesweepers that now crossed the Atlantic to undo the work of their fellow seamen hardly a year before.

In company with her sister ships *Heron*, *Sanderling* and *Oriole* (the Americans customarily named their sweepers after birds), USS *Auk* arrived in

Kirkwall on 29 April 1919 after a two-week passage from Boston. The *Auk* was typical of the minesweepers – 950 tons, just under 188 feet in length, armed with a Lewis gun, and having a crew of 82 men – and some of the incidents in which she and her sisters were involved illustrate the hazards of neutralising mines in the grey, stormy seas between the northern isles and Norway. On 3 May, a boatswain's mate on the *Auk* was fatally injured when he was caught between wire rope and the drum of a winch; as a result, safety guards were installed in all the sweepers. Handling paravanes and sweep wire was an exacting task, with a high risk of accident or fouling, and the *Auk* lost a second man on 31 August off the Norwegian coast when a wire jumped and knocked a boatswain's mate overboard; a one-hour search failed to locate his body.

Added to these dangers was the likelihood of a mine exploding at the wrong moment and setting off counter-explosions in other mines in the vicinity. On the morning of 9 July such an incident took place – a mine exploded and set off a second 25 yards from the *Auk*'s starboard bow and, in turn, this triggered a third 30 yards astern that cut the sweep, causing the loss of the paravane and 70 fathoms of wire. Half an hour later a mine exploded under the *Pelican*, one of *Auk*'s sister ships, and set off five counter-explosions so close to her that the sweeper emerged from the cascade of spray in a battered, listing state. *Auk* immediately came alongside and passed across a line and a hose to assist in pumping, but the heavy sea kept slamming the ships together, tearing the slender threads between them. Another sweeper, *Teal*, managed to pass a line to the *Pelican* and, with the *Auk* and the *Eider* supporting her on either side, began to tow the stricken vessel towards the islands.

The *Pelican* was shipping water fast and began to settle by the head. Commander Bulmer on the *Auk* ordered all but a dozen volunteers to evacuate to the *Eider* and the group of little ships battled onwards, men ready with axes to chop the towlines should the *Pelican* suddenly sink. Gradually the extra pumps and hoses rigged to the *Auk* and the *Eider* began to gain on the water rising inside the *Pelican*. After a day and a night, the ships edged into Tresness Bay on Sanday. The *Pelican* survived her ordeal and was repaired in Scapa Flow before returning to the States in December.

Several other ships involved in the lifting of the barrage suffered damage from mines. The perhaps unfortunately named *Turkey* had to be drydocked at Lyness after a mine exploded almost directly under her. An explosion damaged the *Bobolink* on 14 May and killed her commanding officer, Lieutenant F. Bruce. One of the commandeered trawlers on loan to the United States Navy, the *Richard Buckley*, accidentally hauled a mine that

Fig. 25
Sailors from the United States Navy enjoying some moments with the local girls, possibly in Kirkwall. (Orkney Library)

Fig. 26
*American minesweepers in
Lerwick in May 1919.
(Shetland Museum)*

exploded before it could be jettisoned; the ship went down in seven minutes, with the loss of her captain and six of her crew.

The minesweeping operation shifted to Shetland in August, and the repair ship *Panther* based herself in Lerwick for a month. By the end of September the vital but unglamorous job was complete, and the gallant little ships began to disperse. The base in Inverness had already closed on 17 September. The Royal Navy hauled down its flag in Kirkwall on 1 October, and the last of the Americans sailed for home soon after.[38]

The northern islands found themselves in the front line once again in the Second World War and, to a degree, the strategic situation and the events of 1914–18 were repeated. Between the wars the Royal Navy had shrunk in size according to the limits set in international disarmament treaties, while Germany had in effect no navy until Hitler's regime came to power and clandestinely began to build up armed forces, including a new fleet called the Kriegsmarine. In 1939 when the Home Fleet, the successor to the Grand Fleet, under the command of Admiral Sir Charles Forbes resorted to its main base, an inadequately fortified Scapa Flow, it comprised five battleships, two battle cruisers, two aircraft carriers, fifteen cruisers, some eighteen destroyers and twenty submarines. The German surface fleet included some modern, powerful ships such as the battle cruisers *Scharnhorst* and *Gneisenau*, the heavy cruiser *Hipper*, and the pocket battleships *Graf Spee* and *Deutschland* (renamed the *Lützow* in November 1939). Germany also had fifty-seven U-boats but in other ways was not fully prepared for a war at sea: an aircraft carrier, the *Graf Zeppelin*, was launched in 1938 but was never to be completed, and the battleships *Bismarck* and *Tirpitz* were still in the builders' yards.

A major difference this time round was, of course, the development of air power as a new dimension in naval warfare. The Royal Naval Air Service had been formed in 1912 as an offshoot of the Royal Flying Corps and had made some important advances soon afterwards, a notable one being the first deck landing by an aircraft on a moving ship: on 2 August 1917 Squadron Commander Edwin Dunning touched down his Sopwith Pup on HMS *Furious* in Scapa Flow. Aircraft had been used by both sides for reconnaissance and patrol work but they had played little part in the big-gun battles such as Jutland. During the last months of the War a squadron of Felixstowe F3 flying boats patrolled the Shetland–Fair Isle gap from a base at Catfirth. Two Porte 'Baby' aircraft were also stationed at Catfirth for a time. These lumbering craft had an endurance of six hours and the airmen took carrier pigeons with them, messengers to wing home should the aircraft be down on

Fig. 27

*A 'Baby' Porte seaplane in
Shetland towards the end
of the First World War.
(Copyright IWM.
No. Q 102210)*

the sea and unable to use its suspended wireless aerial. Seaplanes in the
Second World War continued to bring a basket of carrier pigeons on
missions, with fortunate consequences. The main seaplane base in Scapa
Flow was established at Houton. Kite balloons were also used for aerial
observation. A base for two was established at Gremista, on the outskirts of
Lerwick, and at Caldale on the Orkney Mainland, where men would be
winched aloft in a basket, a sometimes perilous undertaking in the northern
winds that met with little success.

The Fleet Air Arm had been formed in 1924 as a branch of the RAF but
it had not been until 1937 that its control passed from the RAF to the
Admiralty, bringing to an end an arrangement that many argued had
inhibited the development of naval air-power. Perhaps it was fortunate, in
retrospect, that German naval air-power never escaped from the tight control
of the Luftwaffe.

An important development in air defence had been the development of
radar, originally a British invention in 1930. By the end of the decade a chain
of radar early warning stations had been created along the eastern seaboard
as far north as Scapa; these could detect approaching aircraft between 80 and
120 miles out, although the range was much less if the aircraft flew low.
Airfields had also been constructed in the islands: Orkney had one Royal
Navy air station, just west of Kirkwall at Hatston, commissioned as HMS

Fig. 28

*Catalina AH551 of 413
Squadron flies over
Bressay Sound.
(Shetland Museum)*

Sparrowhawk; and Shetland was served by the field at Sumburgh Head.
Three more fields were built on the Orkney Mainland during the War:
Skeabrae, built for the Fleet Air Arm but handed over to the RAF in May
1940 for fighter defence; Grimsetter – now Kirkwall airport – which became
HMS *Robin* in 1943; and Twatt, commissioned as HMS *Tern* in April 1941.
Some cautious souls wanted to change the name of the last field as it might
cause unsavoury mirth in the ranks, but this proposal was rejected.

The Sumburgh airfield began its life as a civilian aerodrome. The RAF
acquired it in 1939 and stationed three Gloster Gladiator fighters there.
Situated on a narrow, low-lying strip of land at the southern tip of Shetland,
with the high lump of Sumburgh Head immediately to the south and the
900-foot mass of Fitful Head to the north-west, Sumburgh was a tricky place
for landing and take-off. In 1939, the runways were too short for the most
modern aircraft and, in 1941, they were extended and improved by a
workforce comprising locals and Irish labourers. Before the War, flying boats
from Invergordon searched the Shetland coast for a suitable site for a
seaplane base and found it at Sullom Voe: the Saro London aircraft of 201
Squadron spent some weeks there in the last summer of peace, flew south but

soon returned on 9 August to occupy the Voe as a war station, the home of 100 Wing of 18 Group of Coastal Command. 201 Squadron stayed for three months and was then replaced by 240 Squadron.

Sullom, whose name derives from the Norse for 'sunny home', is a long sea inlet, open to the north and flanked by rolling, bare countryside. Shetland's highest summit, Ronas Hill, broods to the north-west and the island of Yell protects the east side of the approach. At the inner end of Sullom Voe, only a narrow isthmus separates it from Busta Voe where the Northern Patrol found refuge in the First World War. On the east side two smaller inlets, Voxter Voe and Garth's Voe, became anchorages for the seaplanes, and it was around the latter that the shore base for the squadrons sprang up. One obstacle, a rock called Ungam, stuck up in the middle of the voe and aircraft had to avoid it during landing and take-off. Although they generally did, it was to be hit at least three times; once, for example, on a night in January 1942, when a Catalina knocked out the beacon and wrote itself off in the process. At first, there was little in the way of a base on land and headquarters were established on the P&O liner *Manela,* commandeered for the task and moored in the voe. The base was first named RAF Shetland. Construction ashore went on over the winter and the new HQ at Graven began to operate on 17 April 1940. Like their seamen predecessors in 1914, the airmen found Sullom Voe bleak, remote and plagued by wild weather. It was, however, a strategically important station as from here the aircraft could patrol the waters all the way north to the Arctic and west to the Faroes and Iceland, the expected route for the enemy to take to reach the Atlantic.

As a schoolboy at Westsandwick on the east side of Yell Sound, Robert Manson was thrilled by the presence of the RAF. Living under the flight path, as it were, he learned to recognise the various types of seaplane and eagerly absorbed the stories his uncle, who worked at the base throughout the War, brought home at weekends. The ageing Londons and the Sunderlands that replaced them flew on long patrols. The latter had a range of 2,500 to 3,000 miles and stayed aloft for maybe eighteen hours over featureless sea, searching for any sign of a U-boat or lending an extra pair of eyes to watch a convoy in all kinds of weather. Sullom, with its warm food and beds, would have been a welcome place to return to for their crews, but getting back ashore was not always easy. In October 1939 one Sunderland touched down safely in a 60-knot gale but the wind was whipping up the surface of the voe so badly that the crew had to spend another ten hours marooned aboard their aircraft.

In September 1939 a boom was thrown across the entrance to the voe, between Gluss Isle and Calback Ness. The decision was taken to construct a shore airfield at Scatsta beside Garth's Voe; it was to be a satellite station of Sumburgh and provide a base for some fighter protection for the seaplanes. Scatsta, then and still the most northerly airfield in the British Isles, was built over the winter of 1939–40 on a stretch of moorland where some 13 feet of peat had to be scraped away to level the ground for the first runway. The first aircraft to land there, a Hornet Moth bearing an Air Vice-Marshall on an inspection, touched down on 25 April 1940.

The blockade of the North Sea was a central element in naval strategy in 1939, as it had been in 1914. The German response was also a replay of what she had attempted in the First World War – the evasion of the blockade by U-boats and surface ships in order to attack Britain's trade in the open sea. Once again the Northern Patrol went into action and a fleet of twenty-five armed merchant cruisers was earmarked for this service; at the start, however, only three Royal Navy cruisers were available to patrol the gap between the Faroes and Iceland, and a mere two to watch the Faroes–North Rona gap. Vice-Admiral Max Horton was appointed to command the operation, and he hoisted his flag in the cruiser HMS *Effingham*. This was almost too much of a repetition of the past, for the *Effingham* was an old ship in 1939, as the 'Edgars' had been in 1914. The cruisers *Emerald*, *Calypso* and *Dunedin* were also in the patrol force. Once again the contraband control centre was established in Kirkwall but this time the cruisers chose to base themselves in Scapa Flow rather than remote Swarbacks Minn. Horton soon shifted his command base ashore, to a hotel in Kirkwall. In December 1940 he handed over to Vice-Admiral Robert Raikes; Horton was to be appointed to the command of the Western Approaches in November 1942.

Germany had of course anticipated the appearance of the patrol and had dispersed her forces before the declaration of war on 3 September. The *Graf Spee*, the *Deutschland* (*Lützow*) and eighteen U-boats were already at large in the Atlantic; and German merchant ships had been advised to seek haven in neutral ports or try to make their home ports by skirting the Greenland coast far to the north and then dodging down through Norwegian territorial waters. The Northern Patrol intercepted 108 neutral ships in the first three weeks and sent 28 into Kirkwall for inspection. On 9 October, in a gale to the south of Iceland, HMS *Belfast* caught the Hamburg–Süd Amerika liner *Cap Norte* – she had tried to disguise herself as a Swedish ship – and escorted her to Kirkwall; she was seized and converted to a troopship. In November, HMS *Sheffield* intercepted a German freighter, the *Ludolf Oldendorff*, to the west of the Faroes but bad weather prevented boarding

and closer inspection, and the *Sheffield* concluded the ship was neutral and let her go. By the end of the year around a hundred German ships had managed to evade the patrol.

The first winter of the War was a time of trial in several ways for the Royal Navy. On the night of 13–14 October *U-47* slipped into Scapa Flow and torpedoed HMS *Royal Oak* at anchor. For the next six months, until the entrances to the Flow could be secured with blockships and booms, the Home Fleet preferred to seek greater safety in Loch Ewe. Northern Patrol ships shifted their anchorage to Sullom Voe; some of the AMCs had been in Scapa Flow on the night of *U-47*'s attack but, moored close to Flotta, had escaped the enemy's attention. Among the liners commandeered as cruisers and armed with four 6-inch guns was the P&O ship *Rawalpindi*, under Captain E.C. Kennedy. Late on the afternoon of 23 November, in the Faroe–Iceland gap, she spotted an enemy battlecruiser four miles to the west and signalled to Scapa Flow that it was the *Deutschland*, known to be 'out'. In fact it was the *Scharnhorst*. Kennedy steamed to the attack in a hopelessly

Fig. 29
The Scharnhorst.
(Copyright IWM.
No. HU 1042)

Fig. 30

U-47 returns to Kiel to a triumphant greeting from other units of the Kriegsmarine after sinking HMS Royal Oak *in Scapa Flow. The bull painted on the conning tower refers to U-47's nickname after this exploit. (Orkney Library)*

one-sided contest and before the *Rawalpindi*'s companions in the patrol, the cruisers *Newcastle* and *Delhi,* could come to her aid, the German ship's 11-inch guns had battered the liner into a burning hulk. She sank during the night. Only 11 of her crew of 270 survived to be picked up by the Royal Navy; 27 were taken prisoner by their assailant. The *Scharnhorst* slipped away, evaded the Home Fleet units trying to intercept her off Norway and reached Wilhelmshaven. The Admiralty issued a general order to follow and engage enemy ships attempting to escape by entering Scandinavian territorial waters, with the proviso that such action should not endanger civilians.[38]

Early in the war the Luftwaffe turned its attention to the northern islands. The first raid on Scapa Flow took place on 17 October, when two waves of Junkers 88s bombed the base; two of the aircraft were shot down and HMS *Iron Duke*, the floating headquarters of Admiral Sir Wilfrid French, was damaged. Then it was Shetland's turn. The first potential attack came on 7 November but the six aircraft involved were driven off by anti-aircraft fire without apparently dropping any bombs. On the afternoon of 13 November a wave of four Heinkel 111s swooped out of the low cloud over Sullom Voe to be met by a hail of anti-aircraft fire. Four bombs fell in the sea and the rest were dropped, perhaps jettisoned, on the adjoining land where they caused no damage, either plummeting into the soft peat or blasting large holes in the moors and entering history as the first enemy bombs to hit British soil in the Second World War. 'The raid caused some excitement …', noted the *Shetland News*, 'but there was nothing like panic, and a number of people met their first experience of an enemy air raid with almost phlegmatic calmness.'[40]

Among the voe's defences was HMS *Coventry*, a cruiser of 1917 vintage, that had been re-equipped as an anti-aircraft cruiser with ten 4-inch high-angle guns and eight-barrelled pom-poms. One of her complement, George Sims, recalled their first sight of the voe after a stormy passage north: 'Under a sky of brilliant blue, flecked with the tailend clouds of the receding storm, we looked across an expanse of dark water to the stark landscape of crags of varied shapes, and green slopes without a single tree'.[41] On 22 November, six Heinkels came in low over the hills. Driven off by the *Coventry*'s fire, they turned south and attacked the harbour at Lerwick. A London flying boat belonging to 201 Squadron was machine-gunned and set ablaze. Two bombs fell on the Lerwick waterfront, breaking windows and causing some damage to property. In the following weeks, the men in the *Coventry* saw several reconnaissance aircraft fly over their position and, on one occasion, a Heinkel strafed the cruiser's foc'sle. Army units later took over the air defence of Sullom Voe and the *Coventry* left early in 1940.

Over the winter the Shetland aircrews were further blooded. A pilot in

Fig. 31

The craters near Sullom Voe where the first German bombs to hit British soil landed in November 1939. (Shetland Museum)

Fig. 32

Senior army officers survey the Ness of Sound and the southern approaches to Lerwick. In the distance on the left is Bard Head at the tip of Bressay. (Copyright IWM. No. H 18548)

Fig. 33

In the summer of 1940, many Shetlanders volunteered to fill sandbags for the islands' defences. Note that in this photograph the face of the naval officer on the left has been scrubbed out by the censor. (Copyright IWM. No. A 182)

Fig. 34

The Home Guard on
the island of Eday.
(Orkney Library)

Fig. 35

The naval reserve mobilisation notice in a Lerwick post office window in 1939. (Shetland Museum)

240 Squadron lost his life in a Heinkel attack on 19 December, and on New Year's Day 1940 the Sumburgh Gladiators shot down a Junkers 88 east of Fetlar. Towards the end of January the Luftwaffe mounted another small raid on Sullom but it was nipped in the bud by anti-aircraft fire and the Gladiators before any damage was done. On 3 April a Junkers 88 strayed too close to a convoy and a patrolling Sunderland of 204 Squadron shot it down, the first aircraft from Sullom to make a kill.[42]

As in the First World War, Germany relied heavily on iron ore from the far north of Sweden to support her armaments industry and, as in the First World War, when the Baltic froze in the winter, freighters with cargoes of ore steamed through the Inner Leads on the Norwegian coast. The Admiralty, in the person of the First Lord, Winston Churchill, wanted to mine the Leads

but the British government hesitated to breach Norwegian neutrality until the end of March 1940, when it was agreed that mines could be sown in strategic places to force German ships to move offshore. Admiral Erich Raeder, commanding the Kriegsmarine, and his staff had had Norway on their minds since the outset; Admiral Karl Dönitz was attracted by the possibility of bases among the fjords for his U-boats. These would allow Germany to outflank Britain's blockade but Hitler could not be persuaded to invade his northern neighbour. Then the Soviet invasion of Finland and the possibility that the Allies might come to the aid of the Finns via northern Norway and Sweden alarmed Germany. Further concern in Berlin was evoked by HMS *Cossack*'s seizure of the *Altmark* in Jössingfjord inside Norwegian territorial waters on 14 February; this German tanker had been the supply ship of the *Graf Spee*, the raider caught in the Battle of the River

Fig. 37

The 7th Battalion of the Seaforth Highlanders in a convoy of Bren gun carriers on a narrow, misty Shetland road. The 7th Seaforths were garrisoned in the islands between September 1940 and November 1941. (Copyright IWM. No. H 8994)

Plate, and had until the night of her fateful meeting with the *Cossack* cleverly evaded detection in an attempt to reach home with 299 British merchant seamen aboard as prisoners. The German decision to invade both Denmark and Norway was finally taken on 1 March. After a delay caused by ice in the southern Baltic, the German ships were leaving port and heading northward on 8 April just as the British minelayers and their escorts were on their way home from carrying out Churchill's mining plan.

Denmark, threatened with the bombing of Copenhagen, fell within hours but Norway proved a harder nut to crack. For example, coastal batteries sank the heavy cruiser *Blücher* on the approach to Oslo and the Royal Navy's 2nd Destroyer Flotilla fought fiercely against a German destroyer force off Narvik. Royal Navy Skua aircraft from Hatston bombed and sank the light cruiser *Königsberg*, already damaged by Norwegian coastal batteries near Bergen, on 10 April. Surprise, however, favoured the attackers and the major towns were soon in enemy hands. Britain's attempt to mount a counter-invasion by landing troops at Narvik and Trondheim failed. Swordfish aircraft from Hatston launched the first ever torpedo strike against a capital ship when they attacked the *Scharnhorst* on her way back from

Fig. 38

HMS Eskimo *still afloat after her bows were blown off by a torpedo during the second Battle of Narvik on 13 April 1940. The torpedo was fired by the German destroyer Georg Thiele. (Copyright IWM. No. N 233)*

Trondheim on 1 June; the attack failed and two of the Swordfish were shot down. On 8 June, almost a month after German troops had launched their blitzkrieg against Holland and Belgium, the last Allied troops – British, French and Polish – evacuated from Norway. The *Scharnhorst* sank the homeward-bound carrier HMS *Glorious* and two destroyers, *Ardent* and *Acasta*. Two weeks later, on the 21st, another attack against the German battleship failed; Beaufort bombers from 42 Squadron at Sumburgh were intercepted off Bergen and three were shot down in aerial combat with Messerschmitt Bf 109s.

In November 1939 the Admiralty had realised that the fall of Denmark would necessitate immediate steps to establish bases in the Faroes and Iceland to prevent a further outflanking move by the enemy. U-boat and Luftwaffe bases in the North Atlantic would fatally threaten the already fragile convoy lifeline to America. The Faroese were considered by the Royal Navy to be friendly: 'The inhabitants are markedly pro-British and there has been considerable inter-marriage with our trawler crews' reads one minute.[43] It was felt that the Faroese were disenchanted with Danish rule and that they might like to join the Empire with, if not full independence, a status akin to that of the Isle of Man. A plan was hatched to send two officers under the guise of being tourists or fishermen to check out the islands. Winston Churchill, still the First Lord of the Admiralty and defending his turf against accusations of blame for the defeat in Norway, also considered sowing a minefield on the approaches to Bergen, and the seizing and holding of Narvik. These ideas were soon abandoned in favour of the seizure of the Faroes and Iceland.

Communication between the Faroes and Denmark ceased abruptly on the morning of 9 April, but news of the Danish surrender soon reached the islanders by radio; they now felt utterly alone and isolated. There were feelings of resentment over the apparent ease with which Denmark had given in. Three Faroese seamen serving in Danish merchant ships had already been lost to U-boat attack. The islands' parliament, the Løgting, and C.A. Hilbert, the *amtmand* or governor, considered what they should do, their primary concerns being to secure the well-being of their people and keep them supplied with the necessities of life. On 10 April, the *amtmand* announced that his administration would continue, the surrender of the mother country notwithstanding, and agreed to assist Britain. On the following day, the Foreign Office cabled the British consul in Thorshavn to ask the *amtmand* to censor all outgoing wireless and cable messages, suspend the departure of mail, and prepare to receive a force of Royal Marines. Churchill made a statement on the 11th: 'We shall shield the Faroe Islands from all the severities of war.' This message was reinforced by the arrival of two destroyers on the 12th.[44]

The Marines, 250 strong, arrived at three o'clock on the 13th on two armed trawlers, escorted by destroyers and HMS *Suffolk*, in an operation codenamed Valentine. Lieutenant Colonel T.B.W. Sandall, the commanding officer, met the consul, a Mr Lutzen, and the *amtmand* who protested formally against this invasion, the first in the islands' history, apart from a brief seizure of the fort of Skansin by a British pirate in 1808, and then, duty done, immediately became 'most helpful'. The Løgting also protested formally. Generally, however, the Faroese were happy it was the British who had come rather than the Germans. Germany had operated a whaling station at Lopra on the island of Suðuroy and a party of Hitler Youth had paid a visit in 1938, but that seems to have been the extent of pre-War activity. As the marines took up position to defend the strongpoints in the archipelago, British Summer Time was introduced, along with a black-out which, reported Sandall, was taken very seriously. A British envoy, Frederic Mason, arrived to handle relations with the civil authority.

The Admiralty's eyes were on Skálafjord, an 8-mile-long narrow inlet on the island of Eysturoy that had possibilities as a base for capital ships. Surrounded by steep, rugged terrain rising to over 800 feet on the north-west side, the fjord had a narrow, easily guarded entrance. HMS *Franklin* was detailed to make a survey and it was also proposed that HMS *Guardian* should lay anti-submarine indicator nets across the fjord mouth. Permanent protection could be achieved with a boom and a minefield. Admiral Forbes, however, thought Skálafjord had no practical use beyond being a refuelling stop for trawlers and destroyers, and pointed out instead that Iceland would need an anchorage big enough to hold an aircraft carrier if one were to be deployed in the Northern Patrol; he suggested Hvalfjord near Reykjavik, with a subsidiary base for smaller craft at Dyrafjord or Seyðisfjord.

The occupation of Iceland was more fraught than that of the Faroes. Drawing on shared Nordic-Teutonic heritage, Germany had fostered significant cultural links with Iceland in the 1930s whereas Britain had, as usual, neglected her northern neighbours. Also some Icelanders were graduates of German universities. Naval Intelligence warned the Admiralty in March 1940 that immediate steps should be taken to cultivate relations with Iceland – 'nurse' was the verb used – but it was too late now to do much. Intelligence had also minuted that 'Icelanders are rather like their ponies: very obstinate and stiff-necked, and impatient of control', adding that their main desire was independence from Denmark. In 1934 a few Icelanders had proposed their country should join the British Empire but this idea had 'met with no welcome'.[45] Like the Faroese, the Icelanders probably now felt isolated but were unlikely to admit it. Reykjavik had a population of 40,000 at the start of the war and numbered a university and an as yet uncompleted national theatre among its public buildings.

The Icelandic parliament, the Althing, passed two resolutions on the morning of 10 April. These recognised that the Danish king, who was also the king of Iceland, and the Danish government were no longer able to carry out their constitutional duties and that Iceland would therefore govern herself. The British consul in Reykjavik cabled to London the Icelanders' reminder that they had declared permanent neutrality in 1918 and that they would not cooperate with any belligerent power. Iceland reassured Britain of her friendship and hoped that if Britain would respect her neutrality 'other Great Powers' would do likewise, although they admitted that an attack by 'any Great Power' would change the situation fundamentally.

Unease was stalking the Reykjavik streets. Some 110 Germans were in the Icelandic capital, including a large number of seamen from a wrecked ship, and there were fears that they might start something. On the 14th, however, the British consul cabled that the Germans were probably unarmed.

To prevent fights breaking out between the Germans and sailors from Scandinavia, the government imposed a 9 p.m. curfew on all foreign seamen.

The British takeover was codenamed Operation Fork. The occupying force sailed from Greenock for Reykjavik at four in the morning on 8 May: three companies of the Royal Marines and a howitzer battery on HMS *Glasgow*, and a fourth company of Royal Marines with other units on HMS *Berwick*. Two days later, as the cruisers with their destroyer escort edged towards Reykjavik in poor visibility, the *Berwick* launched an aircraft to make a reconnaissance of the harbour; HMS *Fortune* made an anti-submarine sweep through the inner approaches. *Berwick* and *Glasgow* anchored half a mile off, and the troops began to transfer to HMS *Fearless* for the landing. Colonel R.G. Sturges, the commanding officer, reported that inexperience and seasickness caused some delays at this stage. The Marines fanned out through Reykjavik to seize strategic points. Major S.G. Cutler sought out the German consul and wrestled a revolver away from him when he pulled it from his pocket; the consul had started to burn official papers but the fire was extinguished. Some Germans – still drunk from a party the night before – were rounded up and shepherded aboard the *Glasgow*. There was a rush to land stores and the crew of the Hull trawler *Faraday*, which happened to be in port, raised a cheer and pitched in to help their countrymen – 'for no pay', noted Sturges with admiration. The British suffered one casualty: a young Marine on HMS *Berwick* had committed suicide by shooting himself through the heart.

By midday Fork HQ was ashore and, an hour later, a platoon of Marines set off by boat to Akranes, a few miles to the north, to defend Hvalfjord. Sturges met the Icelandic prime minister, Hermann Jonasson, and found him 'pleasant but sad and not communicative'. The chief of police then took Sturges on a car trip around the town – a figurative ride as well as a literal one, the Colonel suspected, when he wasn't shown Havnarfjord, the best landing place, already checked out by the German consul. Sturges also noted that the general population seemed friendly, although a small party of youngsters, who had been hitting the bottle in his opinion, sang 'Deutschland über Alles' in the vicinity of HQ. At five o'clock in the afternoon the *Berwick*, the *Glasgow* and their escort weighed anchor for home, leaving the Marines in possession.

The German occupation of Norway brought the enemy to within 200 miles of Shetland and Britain faced the possibility of an imminent invasion of her sovereign territory. Sea-borne raids on Scapa Flow were expected, the garrison on Orkney was bumped up to 12,000 men, and some women and children were evacuated for a time. In January 1940 Churchill had raised with Sir Dudley Pound, the First Sea Lord, the need to garrison Shetland, and in the spring troopships began to dock in Lerwick to disembark soldiers to defend the islands. Camps, first of tents and then of Nissen huts, sprang up in and around the town. Rows of army huts filled King George V Park, while the navy erected a village of huts on the rounded eminence of the Knab overlooking the southern sea approach. It was estimated that, at the peak, the numbers of service men and women reached almost 30,000.

During March and April, the Luftwaffe flew several bombing raids against Scapa Flow; in the first, on 16 March, Britain's first civilian fatality in an air raid was killed at Bridge of Waithe on the Orkney Mainland. The raids stopped towards the end of April. Incursions by single planes or small groups continued for some time but these rarely resulted in much more than local damage and a test of the defenders' readiness. For example, a pair of Messerschmitt Bf 110s made a low-level attack on Sullom Voe on 23 March 1941 and succeeded in hitting the village before one of them was shot down by the Royal Artillery. The lighthouses in the islands, however, fell victim to more serious air attack on several occasions. The dwelling house at the Fair Isle North light was strafed on 28 March 1941 and attacked again on 18 April when two bombs destroyed some outbuildings. In the following December, Catherine Sutherland, the wife of the assistant lightkeeper, was killed and her infant daughter wounded in an attack on Fair Isle South lighthouse; six weeks later, on 21 January 1942, the wife and daughter of the principal lightkeeper, Willie Smith, met their deaths in a second bombing attack. The Out Skerries lighthouse was bombed on 18 January 1942 and the mother of the boatman was fatally injured.

Apart from the physical dangers from being attacked, the islanders had to live once again with the restrictions imposed by the DORAs. Orkney and Shetland were made a Protected Area on 1 December 1939 and any civilian travelling to or from the islands had to comply with rigorous security procedures. These regulations at times irked the natives, with their customary sense of sturdy independence, but on the whole they understood the necessity and went along with them. From time to time someone would be fined in court for failing to observe the black-out regulations. The editor of the *Orcadian* used the prohibition on outdoor photography to poke some gentle fun at his readership: 'For the duration ... amateurs must forego the little pleasure of camera-recording unique sunsets, fine growths of marrow-stem kale, well-built peatstacks, record-size turnips or potatoes, or prize-inspiring cattle, sheep, pigs or horses'.[46]

After the fall of Norway the amount of merchant shipping to be intercepted by the Northern Patrol dwindled, as there were suddenly fewer neutrals and more ships sailing in convoy. On 7 May the AMC *California* and three armed trawlers were despatched to patrol the east coast of Iceland to spot any enemy move in that direction. German naval intelligence, the B-Dienst, had managed by this time to crack some Royal Navy codes and were able to follow the movements of some of the Northern Patrol ships. Consequently the *Gneisenau* and the *Hipper* were ordered from Trondheim on 22 June to deal with some of the AMCs, but they were spotted by the submarine HMS *Clyde,* who damaged the *Gneisenau* with a torpedo, and they turned back. U-boat attacks on the patrol were more successful and in June both the *Scotstoun* and the *Andania* were sunk. Britain laid more minefields along the route to Iceland and Greenland in July, announcing at the time the channels that civilian shipping was required to follow. Throughout the remainder of 1940 there was a gradual shift of the patrol from the north to the Western Approaches and to the mouth of the Mediterranean. The air raid on Sullom Voe in November 1939 had led Admiral Horton to shift the base of the patrol to Loch Ewe. The shore headquarters moved from Kirkwall to Largs in mid-July and, by mid-December – which saw only fifteen interceptions in northern waters – the AMCs were transferred to Canada and placed under the command of Halifax, where their duties involved patrolling the Denmark Strait and escorting convoys. Hvalfjord became a fuelling point.

Even before the Germans had consolidated their hold on Norway and before the final British evacuation, Norwegian boats began to arrive in the northern isles: yachts and fishing boats, the freighter *Akabahra*, small pleasure craft, even rowboats, sometimes ill-equipped for the risky voyage from the Bergen area, all hijacked or borrowed, all fugitives following in the wake of their Norse forebears a millennium before. On 10 April 1940 the steamer *Bomma* reached Lerwick and the destroyer *Draug* arrived in Sullom Voe, the first Norwegian vessels to escape to the west. The Shetland Bus was on, and the phrase was to become the name for the best-known aspect of Shetland's involvement in the war in the North Atlantic. Eventually over 5,000 Norwegian civilians were to escape to Britain, and around three-quarters of them braved the sea passage. Shetland was the destination and received most of them, but some missed their target. Two boats on separate occasions, one with the Norwegian foreign minister and an admiral aboard, and the other carrying Colonel Dahl, the commander of Norwegian forces north of Narvik, reached the Faroes. Another, the *Svanen*,[47] touched first on Fair Isle and several arrived in Orkney. Each one had an epic tale to tell. In October 1944,

Fig. 39

Four Norwegian refugees from a group who escaped westward in March 1941 and eventually arrived in Westray. The skipper of their boat, Merkur, mistakenly steered north-west for three days until some of his passengers sensed something was odd. Their journey took four days. (Orkney Library)

the *Iwin* suffered an engine breakdown in the middle of the passage, was shot at by a German aircraft, and drifted for nineteen days before a British destroyer found her near Narvik; the air attack had punctured the freshwater tank and the men, who had all fled from forced labour camps and stolen the boat, had survived on rainwater.[48]

The exodus was not a steady stream: 34 boats came in May 1940 immediately on the back of the invasion, and the majority escaped between August and October 1941 when 109 boats made the trip, urged to go by increasingly severe German occupation measures and reprisals. The number of boat attempts dropped when it became slightly easier for refugees to escape overland to Sweden. The last boat to reach Orkney arrived in April 1945. Many never made it, their frail craft foundering in heavy seas, their exact fates unknown, although the total lost has been worked out to be 166. The occupying forces were also on the look-out for escapees: 7 boats were caught, with 77 passengers between them, and the refugees were executed or sentenced to a concentration camp – 321 were killed or died in this way.[49]

The boats are best remembered but aircraft too found an escape route. The first, an MF11 seaplane of the Royal Norwegian Air Force, flew into Lerwick harbour on 12 April, after the three-man crew had run out of ammunition in the battle over the fjords and decided to head west to offer their services to Britain. A week later, an Arado 196 seaplane landed at Sullom with three people aboard. On 9 June, the day before the Norwegians capitulated to the invaders, another four pilots made a break for it, flying three of their own Heinkel 115 aircraft and one captured Luftwaffe

Fig. 40

*Two Norwegian fishing
boats, the* Sjølivet *and
the* Lygrefjord, *moored
at the Malakoff Pier in
Lerwick. Both belonged
to the Shetland Bus and
took part in mine-
laying missions.
(Shetland Museum)*

specimen; one had to ditch in the sea when he ran out of fuel but the other
three reached Sullom Voe safely.

In the winter of 1940–41, as the Free Norwegian forces were assembling
in Britain, some of the men who had escaped in fishing boats were asked if
they would sail back to land agents, equipment and weapons. Some readily
agreed and a nucleus of crews engaged on this dangerous clandestine work
formed in Shetland, choosing their own skippers. The Shetland end of the
operation was placed under the command of Major L.H. Mitchell and early
in 1941 Lieutenant David Howarth RNVR was appointed to assist him.[50]

Mitchell and Howarth searched the much-indented Shetland coast for a
suitable spot for a base and found it at Lunna Voe in the northern Mainland.
Here was a secluded bay, well sheltered and remote, with a quay and a large
country house that could accommodate thirty-five men. The operation was
officially under the control of the Senior Naval Officer in Lerwick but he
seems to have wisely left the crews to get on with things in their own way.
The Norwegian fishermen, all volunteers, were very independent-minded and
contemptuous of higher authority; Howarth says they strongly resented
attempts to bring them under the control and discipline of the Royal
Norwegian Navy.

The first mission took place on 30 August 1941. The cutter *Aksel* under

the command of a young fisherman called August Naeröy carried an agent to make contact with a group of resistance fighters north of Bergen. To look as much as possible like what they pretended to be, the fishermen went to ingenious lengths to camouflage equipment and weapons. Howarth invented a way of concealing pop-up Lewis guns inside oil drums. The *Aksel* chugged out from Lunna Voe as darkness fell over the sea. The crossing should have taken twenty-four hours and she was therefore expected back on 3 September. Howarth records the anxiety at Lunna when she became overdue; and then a Blenheim of Coastal Command sent to look for her spotted her half-way home. It was a valuable lesson – many eventualities could conspire to make the Shetland Bus late. In this instance bad weather had delayed the crossing and had forced a landfall too far south; this had meant the crew had to lie offshore for a day pretending to be ordinary fishermen. A further delay happened because the supposed fishermen were invited to a local dance and then felt obliged to entertain some girl friends. There had been no contact at all with the Germans.

By no means were all subsequent missions to be as pleasant. As the Germans grew more aware of what was going on, they made special efforts to trap the boats; and not all Norwegians could be trusted. Operations always took place in winter – there wasn't enough darkness in summer for

Fig. 41

The Arthur *about to set out from Lunna Voe. Skipper Leif Larsen is second from the left in the foreground group. The three men on the right are agents to be landed in occupied Norway. (Norges Hjemmefront Museum)*

Fig. 42

Four of the Norwegians involved with the clandestine operations of the Shetland Bus. Leif Larsen is on the right. (Norges Hjemmefront Museum)

clandestine voyages – and in itself this meant the risk of exposure to mountainous seas. In November 1941 the *Blia* went down in a storm with all hands – her seven-man crew and thirty-six refugees. Another boat, the *Arthur*, survived that tempest and reached Lunna in a battered, limping condition after fighting the sea for four days.

The *Arthur*'s skipper was Leif Andreas Larsen, the most famous of the Shetland Bus captains. Howarth described this unassuming, brave man as one of the most remarkable people he ever met; his fellow Norwegians agreed with this assessment, for they nicknamed him 'Shetlands' Larsen and gave him more military decorations than any other marine officer. Larsen, who died in 1991, made a total of fifty-two trips across the North Sea with agents, refugees and weapons. There isn't space here to tell of his adventures beyond a brief account of the attack he led on the *Tirpitz* in the summer of 1942.

After the destruction of the *Bismarck* in May 1941, the *Tirpitz* was the only battleship in the Kriegsmarine. Her presence in the Norwegian fjords was a constant threat to the convoys bound for the Soviet Union and her strategic importance naturally meant that she was heavily guarded at all times. Her anchorage 70 miles up Trondheim Fjord had been sited where the surrounding mountains prevented conventional air attack. David Howarth conceived of attempting to approach her with torpedoes slung under a boat, and Leif Larsen was delighted to try it. The original idea was modified, with underwater Chariots being substituted for the torpedoes. Each Chariot was ridden by two men in diving suits and carried an explosive warhead that could be attached to the target and set to go off according to a time fuse. Larsen and three crew in the *Arthur* sailed with the Chariots and their crews towards the end of October 1942. With the Chariots hanging under the hull and six men in hiding aboard, the *Arthur*, ostensibly carrying a cargo of peat up the fjord, managed to penetrate the Germans' security and was only 5 miles from the *Tirpitz* when a stretch of rough water strained the Chariots' towing cables and snapped them. With the Chariots lost to the depths of the fjord, the attack had to be abandoned but now Larsen and his colleagues were faced with how to escape. They decided to land in a remote spot, scuttle the *Arthur* and make their way on foot over the mountains to Sweden. After five days they were only some 10 miles from the border when they were ambushed at night by police and had to shoot their way out of the fix and scatter in the darkness. Over the next few hours they managed to win the safety of Sweden, from where they were able eventually to come back to Britain – all except one, Able Seaman Robert Evans, who was wounded and captured, and then executed.

In the summer of 1942, the Shetland Bus base moved to Scalloway to take advantage of better facilities. Here a slipway, still in use today, was constructed in the engineering works and boatyard of William Moore and Son, and a close collaboration between the local people and their Norwegian guests soon developed. The Norwegians used a nearby sail-loft as a barracks. Flemington House, a mansion at Kergord a short distance north of Scalloway, was taken over as a headquarters for clandestine operations where agents prepared for their hazardous missions.

The first regiment chosen to relieve the Marines who had occupied the Faroes and provide a long-term island garrison was the Lovat Scouts, originally formed as a force specialising in mounted reconnaissance by the sixteenth Lord Lovat, Simon Joseph Fraser, early in 1900 to serve in the Boer War.[51] From a rural Highland background, many of the scouts were already crack shots, skilled in stalking and expert pony handlers. In April 1940 the scouts were encamped in villages in Nottinghamshire as part of the Cavalry Division, training and thinking they were soon to be posted to the Middle East when word came to the commanding officer, Lieutenant Colonel the Honourable Ian Melville, that their overseas destination was to be in entirely the opposite direction. Roddie Campbell, a trooper from Loch Ussie near Dingwall, said the ranks didn't know where they were going but thought it

Fig. 43

Led by their pipe band, the Lovat Scouts march along a quay in Thorshavn. (Copyright IWM. No. H 10537)

might be Norway.

On the foggy morning of 25 May 1940, the steamer *Ulster Prince* eased her way alongside the quay in Thorshavn to the sound of the Lovat Scout pipers. A large crowd of townspeople gathered to see what was going on and stayed all day to watch the disembarkation. The scouts, who numbered 450, settled in, first in billets in schools and other public buildings and then in their own camp of Nissen huts. The rugged terrain of the islands was not easy to guard and the soldiers focused their efforts on defending Thorshavn, Skálafjord to the north, and a few other strongpoints.

Lieutenant Colonel Melville reported to the War Office at the end of June that no German nationals had been found in the islands, although they had identified one Austrian with a pre-*Anschluss* passport, two Hungarians, a few Danes and some people with German links in the family tree. At various times Melville also asked for more troops and heavier guns.[52]

The selection of the Lovat Scouts to be the first foreign troops to garrison the Faroes was an inspired choice. The men came from places where crofting and fishing were the daily norm and where, especially in the Hebrides, the climate was similar to that in the islands. There was every likelihood that the Highlanders would be able to get along with the Faroese, and so, by and

Fig. 44

Some British officers bargain for some dried fish in the Faroes. Eric Linklater, on the right, seems pleased with his purchase. (Copyright IWM. No. H 10581)

Fig. 45

Lovat Scouts on Svinoy. Roddie Campbell at the back. (Roddie Campbell)

Fig. 46
A Lovat Scout patrol out on a Faroese hillside.
(Copyright IWM. No. H. 10568)

large, it turned out. Several married Faroese women. Although there were moments of friction through the requisition of private property and the building of barracks on fertile ground, always a scarce asset in the Faroes, M.L. Melville, the regimental historian of the Lovat Scouts, says the Highlanders 'gained the respect and friendly cooperation' of the islanders.

Roddie Campbell recalls the Faroese as 'really nice people'. On landing, his squad (C Squadron) was sent straight to Toftir on the eastern side of the mouth of Skálafjord where they found accommodation in an empty house. Over the succeeding months the squadrons rotated through a series of postings to different parts of the islands, making sea journeys that tested their endurance of storms. In Sandvik on Suðuroy they were billeted in a school. A trooper from Lewis took over the running of a Norwegian fishing boat, originally called the *Jalso* and renamed *Poppy*, to deliver rations to outlying posts. The men settled into a routine and began to take part in local events, and Roddie Campbell witnessed one of the whale hunts for which the Faroes was famous. Returning from a dance at Lopra, some scouts ignored local advice and wrecked the boat they were using – the kind of event that could just as easily have happened back home. One of the officers told Eric Linklater in 1941 that some of the men were in danger of becoming more Faroese than the natives.[53]

A gun battery was set up to defend the approaches to Thorshavn and the Senior Naval Officer established his headquarters in the old fort of Skansin. The first air attack came at dusk on Friday, 22 November 1940, when one or possibly two – the Admiralty report is uncertain – German seaplanes dropped torpedoes in an attempt to sink a trawler in Thorshavn harbour. The weapons missed their target but the heavy explosions when they struck the coast caused minor damage to the hospital and a few other buildings. There were no casualties. The most serious attack took place on 21 February 1941 and was again directed against the shipping in Thorshavn; on this occasion two Heinkel bombers sank the trawler *Lincoln City* and eight seamen were lost. The Faroese ignored a hail of machine-gun fire and put out in small boats to help the sailors. One of the attackers was hit by Bren gun fire and came down in a fjord. As it sank, the four aircrew rowed ashore in a rubber dinghy to be captured by Trooper J. Mackenzie from South Uist, who disarmed them, gave them some coffee in a Faroese house and then locked them in the school until help arrived.

Relations between occupier and occupied were correct rather than cordial in Iceland. The Icelanders simply did not want foreign troops on their territory but recognised the reason for their presence and had to tolerate them. There

Fig. 47
Lovat Scouts in the Faroes.
(Roddie Campbell)

Fig. 48
Lovat Scouts feeding sheep on Svinoy.
(Roddie Campbell)

Fig. 49

Sandy Sutherland, Lovat Scouts, keeping a watchful eye on Strendur, Faroes. In civilian life, Sutherland was a stalker from Fannich.
(Roddie Campbell)

Fig. 50

Three German Luftwaffe personnel taken prisoner after being shot down by the Lovat Scouts in the Faroes in 1941. The photograph was probably not taken in the Faroes.
(Roddie Campbell)

were some notable exceptions to this attitude but on the whole Eric Linklater's impression when he visited in January 1941 was of a 'frosty indifference' towards the soldiers.[54] Linklater expanded on this point in his postwar book *Fanfare for a Tin Hat*: 'To their surprise and perturbation [the British occupying force] were not welcomed by the inhabitants … The Icelanders … were deeply offended by the invasion … Many … would have preferred a German garrison to ours'.

The British infantry arrived just over a week after the Royal Marines had secured Iceland's strong points. In an operation dubbed Alabaster, the troopships *Franconia* and *Lancastria* steamed into Reykjavik to disembark the 147th Infantry Brigade, comprising the 6th and 7th Battalions of the Duke of Wellington's Regiment and the 5th Battalion of the West Yorkshire Regiment, numbering over 3,900 men with 22 nurses. The commodore of the convoy watched the soldiers land with great relief for he felt the Icelandic port was open to U-boat attack and Lord Haw Haw, the Nazi propagandist, had announced that both transports had been sunk. Two days later Colonel George Lammie took over command of the land forces and the Royal Marines boarded the liners for home. The overall commander (GOC) of the

occupying force was Major-General H.O. Curtis, later to be irreverently
baptised Hoc the Goc by the Canadian troops.[55]

As the occupying force set about assessing the requirements for artillery,
an examination service for ships was opened. Hvalfjord was turned into a
refuelling base and anchorage. From time to time signs of hostility towards
the soldiers emerged: on the evening of Sunday 2 June the Admiralty noted
what it termed a fracas between 'a crowd of roughs and a small party of
NCOs'. There were persistent rumours of German troops landing, for
example at Loðmundarfjord, 15 miles north of Seyðisfjord, on the east coast.
A patrol set off to investigate and a squadron from Scapa Flow, including
HMS *Renown* and HMS *Repulse*, made towards the area at full speed.
Cruisers probed inshore in thick fog to look for signs of the enemy. They
found nothing, as did a Sunderland flying boat from Sullom Voe that
searched along the coast. The Royal Navy interrogated local boat crews,
finally concluding on 8 June that no landing had taken place and that the
rumours had been started by Nazi sympathizers.

'Slowly,' wrote Eric Linklater after the war, '[the Icelanders'] hostility
retreated and grudging tolerance replaced it. For that improvement our

Fig. 51

*The inlet where the
German aircraft was shot
down in the Faroes.
(Roddie Campbell)*

Fig. 52
*Canadian troops pushing a
truck during unloading
operations at Reykjavik
harbour. (Copyright IWM.
No. H 3142)*

Fig. 53

Canadians of the Royals camp beside a road in Iceland where they manned a road block and check post. (Copyright IWM. No. H 3170)

soldiers were responsible. Many were Yorkshire Territorials whose common sense and sturdy geniality quickly recommended them.' The islanders admitted that the troops behaved correctly and eventually 'amicable relations' grew.[56] The West Yorkshires had done well. When they had arrived, lines of men and boys had watched them 'in grim silence', recorded the regimental historian, '[but] the effects of Nazi propaganda soon wore off, and in time the Icelanders became quite friendly to our troops and showed them much hospitality'.[57]

The fear of an attack on Iceland led to reinforcement of the garrison with almost 1,000 men of the Royal Regiment of Canada in June 1940. Churchill balked at a plan to send the whole of the 2nd Canadian Division to Iceland: on 7 July he wrote to the Secretary of State for War that 'it would surely be a very great mistake to allow these fine troops to be employed in so distant a theatre' and that territorial forces should go instead. Apparently he did not receive satisfaction on this point and sent on a hasty memo two weeks later complaining he had had no reply to his query as to why the Canadians were 'being frittered away in Iceland'.[58]

The 1st Battalion of the Tyneside Scottish arrived in Reykjavik as part of the 70th Infantry Brigade in the early autumn of 1940 and found the appearance of the capital with its 'countless lights' an unforgettable contrast with the blacked-out cities they had left behind. The Tyneside Scottish moved into the army camp at Baldurshagi beside a fine salmon river. Their parades in Highland dress, accompanied by the pipes and drums, became, according to their historian, 'the talk of Reykjavik and for once the natives displayed the keenest interest in a unit of the British Army.'[59]

The British forces made detailed plans for a declaration of martial law to be implemented in the event of a German invasion. This did not materialise and the Icelanders were never subjected to a harsh regime. Meanwhile it was recognised that four areas were key to the defence of the country and the Allied war effort: the environs of Reykjavik and Hafnarfjord; the areas around Hunafloi and Akureyri on the north coast; and the Seyðisfjord–Reyðarfjord district in the east. One of the problems faced by the defenders was the long distances between these places and the nature of the roads – gravel and mud in summer, and liable to blockage with snow in winter, when the garrison in Seyðisfjord could be reached only by sea. Akureyri, the second largest town, lay beside a fjord at the end of a long, rough road from Reykjavik. The road was held to be impassable in winter, there was no airfield apart from an uneven stretch of stone and lava 20 miles away, and the harbour was, in the Admiralty's opinion, good only for small trawlers, although the mail steamer and small cargo boats did use the jetty.

Fortunately the fjord was ideal for seaplanes. The town had one main street, a good water supply, hydro-electricity, three hotels and three schools where forty soldiers could be billeted.

The soldiers therefore had to cope with reluctant hosts and an adverse environment. The Canadians, who knew a thing or two about hard winters, provided the troops with huskies for dogsleds but the British treated them as pets and found they no longer did their work. The defence network included forty-three coastwatching posts, most of which were manned by the Royal Navy, although the Army looked after some and one was the responsibility of the Royal Norwegian Navy. The Army liked to rotate its men every fortnight but the Navy preferred its personnel to stay in post for long periods to get to know the local fishermen. Four sailors from HMS *Suffolk* landed in May 1941 to set up a coastal watch at a remote settlement in the north-west; they were 40 miles from the nearest shop and cut off from the rest of Iceland by cliffs and steep hills, but three of the four volunteered to live in this spot for the duration of the War (Fig. 62).

Iceland was too far from Norway for the Luftwaffe to mount many air attacks, although long-range reconnaissance aircraft were sometimes daily seen overhead. A platoon of the Tyneside Scottish was strafed by a solitary

Fig. 54

A sailor and a soldier survey the Reykjavik seafront. The building with the spire is the Catholic church. (Copyright IWM. No. H 3319)

attacker at Selfoss in 1941 while on their way to church parade – one man was killed – and Seyðisfjord was bombed twice in the summer of 1942, four children being injured on one occasion. On 10 February 1944 a Focke-Wulf Condor bombed and sank the British tanker *El Grillo* in Seyðisfjord harbour; there were no casualties but 9,000 tons of oil escaped to cause a considerable pollution problem.

Both the Faroes and Iceland had a range of political parties and their people took an active interest in politics. An election in the Faroes in January 1940 had resulted in a fairly even spread of seats across the islands' party spectrum: the twenty-four seats in the Løgting were divided between the *Sambandsflokkurin* or Unionists (eight seats), the Social Democrats (six), the *Folkaflokkurin* or People's Party (six) and the *Sjalvstyri* (four). The latter two were in favour of home rule and were given a boost by the occupation which brought considerable prosperity and showed that the islands could go it alone.

Parties in Iceland comprised the Conservatives, the Progressives, Socialists and Communists, and a small nationalist party, the *Thjodveldisflokkur*, which emerged during the War. The voting system was structured in favour of the sparsely populated rural constituencies with the result that in the 1938 election the Progressives had won nineteen out of the forty-nine seats in the Althing with only 25 per cent of the popular vote, whereas the urban-based Conservatives had attracted 45 per cent of the vote but had gained only seventeen seats. A coalition government under Hermann Jonasson had been formed in 1939.

Icelandic politicians generally went along with the occupation and the press observed a gentleman's agreement not to mention military matters, all, that is, except the communist paper *Thjodviljinn* who not only objected strongly to the presence of the foreign force but also helped to distribute leaflets urging the troops to disobey orders, especially when servicemen did work during a civilian strike in January 1941. Major-General Curtis closed down the paper in April 1941 and deported the editors to Britain, after checking his action with London and the Icelandic government. The latter said they would rather he did it than leave them with the task of prosecuting the editors under the country's treason laws, particularly as forthcoming elections prevented them from curbing the freedom of the press. When American troops arrived in 1942, the editors came back and one of them, Einar Olgeirsson, joined a new communist paper, where he attacked Britain for not opening a second front to help the Soviet Union. He stopped his attacks once he learned of the Arctic convoys and the aid being passed to Stalin. Relations with the Iceland government suffered for a time after the British minister, Howard Smith, died suddenly in July 1942.[60]

Fig. 55
Townspeople gather in Akureyri as a troopship leaves the quayside. (Copyright IWM. No. H 3840)

Fig. 56

*Troops of the West Yorkshire Regiment exercising with a 3-inch mortar in Iceland.
(The Yorkshire Post, and the Prince of Wales Own Regiment of Yorkshire Museum)*

Fig. 57

*Mail arrives in an Iceland army camp.
(The Yorkshire Post, and the Prince of Wales Own Regiment of Yorkshire Museum)*

Fig. 58

*Troops of the West Yorkshire Regiment exercising in the rugged Iceland landscape.
(The Yorkshire Post, and the Prince of Wales Own Regiment of Yorkshire Museum)*

When Denmark fell under Nazi occupation, the local government in Greenland, part of the Danish realm, asked for America's protection and the US Coastguard cutter *Comanche* was despatched to Ivittuut (Ivigtut) with a diplomatic representative.[61] Germany had already established weather-forecasting bases on the long, frozen eastern coast fronting the Denmark Strait and intelligence early in 1941 suggesting that plans were afoot to add an air base prompted America to act. A party from the Royal Norwegian Navy ship *Fridtjof Nansen* had occupied one district in September 1940, and Canada had expressed her willingness to put troops into Greenland to protect a cryolite mine at Ivittuut if her southern neighbour were unable to act. The administration of President Franklin Roosevelt, pushing the boundaries of neutrality, reached an agreement with the Danish minister in Washington on 9 April 1941 whereby the USA would take over the defence of Greenland. The Americans soon began to construct bases for aircraft and communications, all to become known as 'Bluies'. On 7 May HMS *Somali* captured a German weather ship.

With the occupation of Greenland, the last link in the chain of land masses flanking the great circle route, the shortest distance across the North Atlantic from Europe to America, was in place, with important consequences for the protection of the Atlantic convoys, the supply lifeline on which Britain depended and which was now under great threat. As the German occupation of France had provided Grand-Admiral Karl Dönitz's U-boats with open access to the Atlantic, the enemy no longer had to negotiate the Scotland–Iceland gap to reach their quarry. Dönitz also introduced the tactic of attacking convoys with 'wolf packs' of submarines. In the first six months of the war Britain lost 743,802 tons of merchant shipping or 172 individual vessels, about half of the total to U-boats; between June and December 1940 the losses soared to almost 1,715,200 tons, with a further loss of 743,000 tons of Allied and neutral shipping.[62] In the worst month for Britain – October – losses totalled 352,000 tons. Ships were being sunk at a rate two or three times faster than they could be replaced.

Germany also deployed surface raiders to attack Allied commerce. In October 1940 the pocket battleship *Scheer* and the cruiser *Hipper* passed undetected through the Denmark Strait and attacked a convoy from Halifax accompanied by the AMC *Jervis Bay*, the only escort, whose gallant defence, which ended in her own sinking, allowed the escape of most of the merchant ships. Operating alone, the *Scheer* proceeded to sink more ships in the Indian Ocean before returning home through the Denmark Strait in March 1941. The *Bismarck*, the most powerful capital ship of the time, made her break out into the Atlantic with the cruiser *Prinz Eugen* in May 1941 through the

Denmark Strait. HMS *Hood* and HMS *Prince of Wales* sped westward from Scapa Flow to intercept, and the four ships met in battle to the south-west of Iceland early on the morning of the 24th. The encounter ended quickly when the *Hood* received a catastrophic hit in one of her magazines, blew up and sank with all hands except three. The *Bismarck* escaped, damaged though she had been by gunfire from the *Prince of Wales*, and became the target of a desperate hunt by the Royal Navy that ended with her being battered to a hulk by Home Fleet units on the 27th, leaving 110 survivors from her crew of 2,000. The *Prinz Eugen*, which had parted company with the *Bismarck* after the sinking of the *Hood*, developed engine trouble and returned to port in France without doing any damage to shipping. Other raiders operated mainly outside the area of the North Atlantic where the main enemy remained the U-boat.

Bases in Iceland and Greenland allowed the extension of air cover for convoys into the northern part of the wide gap between the limits air cover could reach from the Canadian and British shores, as well as anchorages where the hard-pressed escort ships of the Royal Navy and the Royal Canadian Navy could find fuel and supplies. Reykjavik became a very busy port with every possible berth in use and America came forth with funds to expand the facilities. Moorings at the fleet base at Hvalfjord were also improved; ships were prone to drag ashore here when violent squalls bored down the mountain valleys. HMS *Argus* brought a party to Reykjavik in

Fig. 61

Ski troops of the West Yorkshire Regiment exercising near Budareyri in Iceland. (Copyright IWM. No. H 9598)

August 1940 to begin work on a Fleet Air Arm base, flying Walrus seaplanes for anti-submarine operations, at Fossvogur in Skerjafjord. The RAF established an airbase at Kjaldadarnes. Outlying air bases were set up at various places around the long coastline, including Búðareyri in Reyðarfjord, Hornafjord, Akureyri and Isafjord. The British troops laboured during the long summer days on the building of the airfields. Escort groups and an anti-submarine striking force began to operate from Hvalfjord at the end of March 1941 and put a further strain on the capabilities of the port. A local firm, Messrs Hamar, was contracted to carry out engineering repairs. A Combined Services HQ was set up at Artun where the Army already had its headquarters.

In May 1941 C. Howard Smith, the British envoy, reported fears among the Icelanders that the new airfield at Reykjavik would be attacked by German bombers. Six Hurricanes were sent to reinforce the existing complement of five Hudsons and a few Battles, and beef up the air defence of the capital. Until 1 July 1941 the maritime defence of Iceland remained the responsibility of the Home Fleet, but on that date it was made an independent command, with Rear Admiral Richard Scott being appointed Admiral Commanding in Iceland (ACIC).

Fig. 63
The first American troops arrive in Reykjavik in 1941 to be greeted by men of the Tyneside Scottish regiment. (author's collection)

Fig. 64
American troops unloading supplies and vehicles in Reykjavik. (author's collection)

Fig. 65

The Northern Lights play in the Iceland sky above a camp of Nissen huts. (author's collection)

In April 1941, America extended her patrols into the Atlantic to waters up to the line of 26°W and warned 'aggressor nations', as Churchill recorded, that the presence of their units in this 'Western Hemisphere' would be made public. On 10 April, the destroyer USS *Niblack* had picked up three boatloads of survivors from a torpedoed merchant ship when she was threatened by a U-boat and drove it off with a depth-charge attack in the first hostile encounter between the American and German navies. Patrolling was about as far as Roosevelt could go without declaring war on Germany. Although the 26° line of longitude ran a short distance beyond the west coast of Iceland, the President proposed in June establishing a US base there and taking over the defence of the country. Admiral King, United States Navy, redefined the Hemisphere in July to include Iceland. C. Howard Smith laid this plan before the Icelandic government and negotiations over the exact wording of an agreement ensued. The Icelanders balked at the use of 'invite' and settled on the phrasing 'are ready to entrust the protection of Iceland to the United States'. This formula was also acceptable in Washington DC, where Roosevelt had to contend with his own political opponents.

The Americans arrived on 7 July in the form of a strong squadron made up of the battleships USS *New York* and *Arkansas*, two cruisers and twelve destroyers, escorting a convoy of eight ships with 4,000 marines, to be

Fig. 66

Norwegian airmen of RAF Coastal Command provide an aerial ambulance for an elderly Icelandic lady. (author's collection)

greeted by the pipeband and a guard of honour from the Tyneside Scottish. Rear-Admiral Scott met his American opposite number, Rear-Admiral David McDougal Le Breton, and recorded: 'He is very pleasant and perhaps the most loquacious person I have ever met.' British troops gradually withdrew from Iceland in 1942 but the Navy and the RAF remained. Some 9,000 more American troops under Major-General C.H. Bonesteel arrived in April and May that year to augment the garrison and relieve the British units. The US Marine Corps soon nicknamed the Hvalfjord base 'Valley Forge' and set up their own at Alafoss, 15 miles inland; disparagingly they coined the term 'Rinkydink' for the Iceland capital.

Scott's report to the Admiralty at the end of July 1941 recorded how life was becoming busier than ever. He also included a summary of shipping events in the first half of the year and these illustrate the difficulties faced by the occupying forces. At the end of December the boom defence vessel HMS *Barrhead* had run ashore east of Vik and anyone attempting to reach her had to slog on horseback through 70 miles of snow; salvage wasn't finally accomplished until the following May by local farmers. Attempts to save the armed trawler *Eduard Van Vlaenderen* after she went ashore in an exposed position at the mouth of Eyjafjord had to be abandoned. The Army had run out of coal and had had to borrow 3,000 tons from the Navy. The Norwegian

Fig. 67

The aircrew in Iceland who attacked a U-boat after only three minutes into their operational flight. On the left is Sergeant Eastwood from Southport, Lancashire. The other four men are Canadian. In the centre is Sergeant Victor Miettinen, the skipper. (Copyright IWM. No. CH 11601)

Fig. 68

Swordfish being loaded with 100-pound anti-submarine bombs at Hatston airfield in 1941. (Orkney Library, Lamb Collection)

Navy had landed a small force on Jan Mayen on 18 May and a regular wireless link had been established with that remote island beyond the Arctic Circle. Two Norwegian freighters had fallen victim to U-boat attack; an Iceland trawler, the *Reykjaborg*, bound for Fleetwood with a cargo of fish, had been sunk in March but another torpedoed trawler, the *Frodi*, had managed to limp back to Reykjavik. Some ships had also been sunk by aircraft while three had disappeared without trace – the Norwegian *Borgund*, the Swedish *Goteborg*, and the Dutch *Texelstroom* which Scott thought had probably gone down with all hands in a hurricane in February while bound for Scrabster. The strong magnetic disturbances in the vicinity of the Iceland coast combined with the stormy, thick weather to make navigation extremely difficult. In the middle of June, a Norwegian fishing boat, the *Aud*, had sailed into Akureyri, after crossing from Narvik with nine refugees and valuable information on enemy forces in northern Norway. HMS *Hecla* had arrived in July to serve as a depot ship for repairing escorts. Static coastal defences had been enlarged to include anti-submarine loops, patrols, booms, a minefield and gun batteries. Scott also noted that a Nazi agent, August Lehrman, had finally been arrested near Isafjord after being in hiding for a year; the seven locals who had helped him were deported to Britain.

The attitude of the Icelanders remained, in Scott's opinion, 'friendly but not cordial'. There were signs that, with the arrival of the Americans, the feelings of antipathy towards the better-behaved British lessened. Good relations had sprouted particularly in the rural districts and the imminent appearance of Americans in these places was not being looked forward to.

Fig. 69

The Norwegian freighter Faro was torpedoed by a U-boat fifteen north-east of Copinsay on 27 January 1941. She drifted ashore at Taracliff Bay on the east side of the Orkney Mainland where she was photographed on the following day by an Anson of 269 Squadron from Wick. Seven men out of her crew of fifteen were lost. (Orkney Library)

Fig. 70

Winston Churchill gives the thumbs-up to a welcoming crowd in Reykjavik on 19 August 1941. (Copyright IWM. No. H 12873)

Fig. 71

HMS Duke of York ploughing through heavy seas in a 60-knot north-easterly gale in March 1942, while defending the convoy route to Russia. The picture was taken from the aircraft carrier HMS Victorious. *(Copyright IWM. No. A 8143)*

The newcomers were very sensitive to this and cracked down hard on offenders in their ranks. The commander of a new US destroyer was summarily dismissed from his ship and sent home after he caused a disturbance in a Reykjavik hotel.

Winston Churchill visited Iceland on his way home from his conference with Roosevelt in August 1941. HMS *Prince of Wales*, with the Prime Minister aboard, reached Hvalfjord on the 16th where, Churchill noted, he 'received a remarkably warm and vociferous welcome from a large crowd'. Later in the day, on the way to paying his respects to the Icelandic government, he experienced cheering and applause in the streets of Reykjavik such as 'seldom have been heard [there]'.

The ranks had an uncomfortable time in 1941. Morale was good in the Navy although their living conditions remained rough and overcrowded while a shore camp was being prepared. Officers in the meantime shared exorbitantly priced hotel rooms with poor service and no public areas, reported Rear-Admiral Scott in December. The local amenities were considered to be poor. Apart from two NAAFI canteens, the YMCA, Toc H and other standard facilities, there were only two small cinemas in Reykjavik

and the small dance halls were off limits to service personnel. Scott's successor, Rear-Admiral Frederick Dalrymple-Hamilton, noted in the middle of 1942 that the naval camp was at last nearly ready. The Canadian beer supplied to the men was apparently stronger than British beer and had caused some 'unseemly drunken occurrences'. The ACIC lived in a house – 22 Tjarnagata, Reykjavik – but, as the Icelandic owner wanted his property back and it was thought politic to accede to this request, he had to move into new quarters. It took longer to prepare the so-called Admiral's Cottage than anticipated, and the final move, by which time Dalrymple-Hamilton had been replaced, did not occur until April 1943. The cottage, in reality a Nissen hut painted a handsome white to give it some distinction, lost its roof three times to blizzards before it could be finished. Finally this problem was solved by the use of 'heavy cordage' to anchor each section of the building until the whole structure was complete. Some 40 tons of concrete were used to clad it, and this was reckoned to be enough to hold it in place.

In December 1941 a regular convoy service began to operate between Britain and Reykjavik, under the code letters UR and RU for outward and inward-bound trips. The convoys continued until May 1945, by which time

Fig. 72

Convoy PQ17 assembling at Hvalfjord in May 1942, seen from HMS Wheatland, a destroyer escort. (Copyright IWM. No. A 8953)

Fig. 73

The Mary Luckenbooth,
*with a cargo of
ammunition, explodes in
convoy PQ18 on 14
September 1942.
(Copyright IWM.
No. A 12271)*

over 160 had sailed in both directions. Convoys also crossed regularly between Reykjavik and the USA.

Units of the US Navy provided escorts for British-bound convoys as far as Iceland. One of these ships, the destroyer USS *Reuben James,* guarding convoy HX156, was torpedoed by *U-562* early on the morning of 31 October 1941 and went down with 115 of her crew to become the first American ship to be lost to enemy action in the war. After the German invasion of the Soviet Union on 22 June 1941, Iceland became the assembly point for convoys carrying war materials to the Russians. The first sailed on 21 August 1941 and by the time this supply route was closed at the end of the war forty-one had made the hazardous outward journey. The Arctic convoys – codenamed as PQ and QP until December 1942 and thereafter as JW and RA – became notorious not only for the dangers from enemy attack but for the numbing cold, the fierce weather and the drabness of Russian ports. In the summer the convoys hugged the Greenland coast as much as possible before striking across past Jan Mayen and Spitsbergen on the 2,000-mile voyage; but in winter the advance of the Arctic pack ice forced them to sail further south and east, setting off from Loch Ewe and passing well within the range of enemy aircraft operating from Norway. Escort vessels had to refuel at sea, often in dirty weather, and the threat from shore-based aircraft prevented the Home Fleet from risking heavy ships east of Bear Island. An Admiralty report at the end of the war concluded that there had never been enough escort carriers available to make the route 'a practicable and sound operation'. Nevertheless the convoys sailed. The first two ships to be torpedoed were hit in PQ8 in January 1942: the *Harmatris* was able to make port but HMS *Matabele* went down with a heavy loss of life.[63] Losses were to grow to alarming proportions very soon after this.

The Faroes acquired their first airfield in 1942. Finding a suitable site, with a sufficient area of relatively level terrain, was no easy task in the mountainous islands and in the end only one place could accommodate the runways – the western shore of the lake called Sörvágsvatn on the island of Vágar. A short distance to the west was Sörvágsfjord, and both the fjord and the lake could be used by seaplanes. Apart from the obvious advantage in having another operational base in the North Atlantic, it was felt an airfield would do much to restore Allied prestige among the Faroese. The islands had experienced forty-six bombing attacks over the winter of 1941–42; lighthouses had been strafed – on 3 April 1942 the Luftwaffe machine-gunned the Akraberg lighthouse on the southern tip of Suðuroy and cracked the lens[64] – and there had been considerable damage to shipping. The fishing fleet was bearing heavy losses.

A large contingent of officers descended on Vágar in March to inspect the site and caused a slight panic, leading some families to move from the island to neighbouring Streymoy for fear of the increased risk of living in the vicinity of such an obvious target. Vágar was to be declared a prohibited area. The Army and the RAF disagreed over details of the airfield design but the RAF's views prevailed.[65] In April RAF Coastal Command also took over the responsibility for the air defence of the Faroes, although the most senior naval officer remained in operational command and dealt with the *amtmand*. Thorshavn, the Navy refuelling station in Skálafjord, the town of Klaksvik, and the new airfield on Vágar were the four main sites to be defended. RDF warning stations were established on the island of Nolsoy, at Akraberg, at Eiði in the north, and on Mykines to the west so that their seaward arcs of coverage overlapped to throw up a complete early-warning screen around the islands.

Group Captain L.G. Maxton took charge of the construction of the airfield. Around 2,000 men from the Pioneer Corps moved into a camp of Nissen huts, and were assisted by a further 300 Faroese workers. Vágar's normal peacetime population was only around 1,500 and there was at the beginning only one road on the island, 10 feet wide with a shingle surface. One of the first tasks was to widen and tarmac this highway. A boat with supplies began to run between the island and Aberdeen every fortnight. Group Captain Maxton thought some of the security measures were ridiculous, as in his view the Germans probably knew exactly what was going on, and he was asked to cease evading censorship by sending letters on any handy boat bound for Aberdeen. He probably needed the sense of humour he showed in his reports: he brought in some fir trees from Scotland and noted in June that some were showing signs of survival although 'fir trees are funny things'. Work progressed well and the airfield 'opened' on 8 June. The first aircraft, a Sunderland that had come up from Invergordon, landed at 3 p.m. on 16 July, and a Catalina flew in from Sullom Voe a week later.[66]

In May 1942 the Lovat Scouts were relieved by the 12th Battalion of the Cameronians (Scottish Rifles) under the command of Lieutenant Colonel C.O. Mackley. The replacement of the now-familiar Lovat Scouts with new soldiers worried the islanders but soon the newcomers settled in and relations between the occupied and the occupiers stayed on a friendly footing. The Cameronians found the rugged islands to be an excellent training ground and also took part in such social events as the inter-village sports. The Battalion quit the islands in August 1943, relieved by the South Staffordshire Regiment. During their stay the Battalion historian noted that it was hard to

Fig. 74
The Finnish steamer
Carolina Thorden *on fire*
after being bombed in
Faroese waters in March
1941. One of the Faroese
rescue boats is in the
foreground.
(Copyright IWM.
No. K 215)

Fig. 75

A Catalina seaplane beached on rocks on Whalsay, September 1942. (Shetland Museum)

Fig. 76

A radar operator, Leslie Neal, from the RAF station at Netherbutton, practises his piping during a visit to RAF Deerness. (Orkney Library)

keep morale up with too little daylight in winter and too much in summer; and the term 'Faroitis' was coined for the depression he says sometimes afflicted the men.[67]

On 18 February 1943 gale-force winds reached 100 miles per hour at the Vágar airfield, blew down the 90-foot timber mast of the VHF station and destroyed one of the technical huts near its base. Nowhere along the North Atlantic Front did anyone need reminding that damage to limb and property was more likely to be perpetrated by the elements than by the enemy. Many aircraft and aircrews were lost through accidents in bad flying conditions,[68] and some shipping losses in storms have already been noted. The occupation of Iceland and Greenland provided access to meteorological data that became crucial to the planning of some Allied operations but for most of the military personnel the weather was just something else that had to be put up with. There was a good deal of boredom associated with routine garrison duties and patrolling. Like many bases, Vágar had its programme of entertainments: these were the delights on offer in one week in December 1943:

Fig. 77

The base at Graven sprawls around the shores of Sullom Voe. (Shetland Museum)

3.12	Cinema in dining hall *Between Us Girls*.
4.12	Darts competition in recreation room.
5.12	ENSA concert in dining hall.
6.12	Whist drive in recreation room.
7 and 8.12	Cinema in dining hall *Wake Island*.
9.12	Talk and discussion on Faroes by F/O Nettleton.

Fig. 78

Captain H. St J. Fancourt, the commanding officer of Hatston airfield, with perhaps the most famous star to entertain the troops in Orkney, Gracie Fields, in July 1941. Gracie Fields and George Formby were among the stars who also performed at the Garrison Theatre in Lerwick. (Orkney Library, Lamb Collection)

The Allies struck back at the Nazi regime in Norway in a series of raids and combined operations. Some were on a small scale, involving only handfuls of the newly formed British Commando force and other units: such were the attacks on the hydro-electric plant at Glomfjord in 1941 and the pyrites mine on the island of Stord in January 1943 which is described later. On 3–4 March 1941, Commando and Norwegian forces in two infantry landing ships escorted by five destroyers sailed from Scapa Flow and launched a surprise raid codenamed Operation Claymore on four towns in the Lofoten islands. They came away with over 200 prisoners and over 300 Norwegian volunteers, including eight women and the much relieved manager of an English business firm. The raiders sank five ships and left behind devastated factories and blazing fuel tanks. No. 12 Commando made a second assault on the southern part of the Lofotens just after Christmas that same year, in Operation Anklet. Distant Spitzbergen, 370 miles beyond the North Cape,

Fig. 79

The congregation of the church on Westray turned out in their Sunday best on 25 April 1943 to recover this crashlanded Grumman Wildcat. (Orkney Library, Lamb Collection)

Fig. 80
RAF personnel and
civilian guests enjoying a
hut party at Graven camp
beside Sullom Voe.
(Shetland Museum)

was raided by a combined force of Norwegian, Canadian and British units in
August 1941; the coal mines were put out of action and the inhabitants, who
included some 2,000 Russian miners, were evacuated. No. 12 Commando
and the Royal Norwegian Army landed again on Spitzbergen on Boxing Day
1941, when the German garrison was still recovering from its Christmas
festivities, and destroyed two wireless stations.

The largest raid, Operation Archery, targeted the island of Måløy and the
adjacent town of Vågsøy, on the island of the same name, at the mouth of
Nordfjord. This strategic point on the west coast, where shipping using the
Inner Leads had to emerge in the open sea to double the Stadlandet
peninsula, was heavily fortified with anti-aircraft and field artillery. The
raiding force, led by the cruiser HMS *Kenya*, sailed from Scapa on the
afternoon of Boxing Day 1941 and opened the attack just before 9 o'clock
the following morning with a burst of star shell that split the winter darkness
above Måløy. While the Navy bombarded the settlements and dealt with
ships in the surrounding waters, army units landed at four separate locations
and the RAF bombed installations and defended against the Luftwaffe's
attempts to disrupt the attack. The Germans recovered quickly from the

initial shock to put up a spirited defence. Vicious house-to-house fighting developed in the streets of the small town and the Norwegian Captain Martin Linge was killed during the assault on the German HQ. By midday, however, the Allies had prevailed and late in the afternoon withdrew with their prisoners, leaving costly destruction in their wake.

These raids had strategic consequences far beyond their immediate tactical effect: they boosted Norwegian morale and convinced Hitler that he had to fear an invasion of Norway, against which a garrison of up to 400,000 German troops had to be maintained.

The most contested arena, and the most strategically significant, remained the Atlantic Ocean itself. On 9 May 1941, during an attack on convoy OB318, *U-110* was captured intact by the escorts, and a boarding party from the destroyer HMS *Bulldog*, led by Sub-Lieutenant David Balme, secured an Enigma coding machine and codebooks. The *Bulldog*'s attempt to tow the U-boat to Scapa failed and she had to be left to sink, but this freed the destroyer to refuel at Reykjavik and race to Scapa Flow with the key to German naval codes. Although the decoded intelligence had to be used with

Fig. 82

British and Norwegian troops evacuating civilians from a dangerous area in Vågsøy in December 1941. (Copyright IWM. No. N 497)

Fig. 83
A fish-oil factory ablaze during the raid on Vågsøy in December 1941. In the foreground commandos watch for snipers or a counter-attack.
(Copyright IWM. No. N 459)

care so as not to give the game away, this lucky break enabled the Allies to track the enemy's movements, re-route convoys to avoid the wolf packs and attack U-boat supply ships. German Intelligence sensed that their security had been breached but never got to the bottom of what had really occurred.

Later in the year the Allies captured another U-boat and this time did not lose her to the sea. On 27 August a Coastal Command Hudson of 269 Squadron was on patrol some 80 miles south of Iceland when its crew spotted *U-570* on the surface. The Hudson, piloted by Squadron Leader J. Thompson, dived to the attack and released four depth charges before coming round again to strafe the vessel. The German crew and their captain, Commander Hans Rahmlow, surrendered; the initial depth-charge attack had apparently caused enough damage to prevent the vessel submerging. Thompson and his men circled overhead, threatening to open fire should the enemy try to scuttle, until a Catalina flying boat relieved them. Later in the day an armed trawler towed the U-boat to the beach near Thorlákshöfn on the south coast. Here she lay in the breaking surf for six days while a team of seamen worked in the oily, dark interior to make her seaworthy. She was found not to be as badly stricken as her German crew had thought. Some of her equipment, including the Enigma machine, had been destroyed to prevent it falling into enemy hands but the vessel herself was in eminently good condition, and impressed the Royal Navy men with her facilities. Finally afloat, she was towed west to HMS *Hecla* for final repair. On 29 September *U-570* set off for Britain and arrived in Barrow-on-Furness four days later, where she was to be renamed HMS *Graph* and used for training.[69]

Despite such successes and the falling rate of loss of merchant shipping, the battle remained finely poised. The U-boats were having trouble finding the convoys but equally the escorts couldn't locate the U-boats, whose numbers were actually increasing: Dönitz had 200 by the end of 1941. In the first half of 1942, the U-boats had more success, sinking over 3,300,000 tons of shipping in the North Atlantic, losses partly brought about by the reluctance of the Americans, now in the War, to impose convoy traffic along their east coast. At last, towards the end of 1942, shipyards began to launch more tonnage than was sunk. Thereafter the pendulum swung between favouring the Allies one month and the raiders the next. The struggle reached a crux in March 1943 and then the Allies' gradual development of better tactics, and provision of more escorts and increased air cover began to tell, and tell relatively quickly. On 24 May Dönitz transmitted the order to his U-boat skippers at sea to quit the North Atlantic for better hunting south-west of the Azores.

The convoys to the Soviet Union likewise had to endure heavy losses in

1942. Of the thirty-five merchant ships in PQ17, which sailed from Iceland on 27 June, only eleven arrived in the safety of Russian waters. Uncertainty over the location of the *Tirpitz* and other German surface ships led the Admiralty to issue a series of confusing orders that resulted in the withdrawal of the escorting cruisers and the scattering of the convoy. U-boats and aircraft now made the most of an easy opportunity to pick off the ships. In September PQ18 lost thirteen ships, mostly to bombers.

On the last day of 1942, convoy JW51B became the focus of a sea fight that had important consequences for the Kriegsmarine. Known to the Royal Navy as the Battle of the Barents Sea, it began when Vice-Admiral Oskar Kummetz sailed from Altafjord in command of the cruiser *Hipper* to lead an attack on the convoy which, at that moment, was steaming east past Bear Island towards Murmansk. Kummetz's force also comprised the pocket battleship *Lützow* and six large destroyers. Escorting the convoy were eleven destroyers and escorts, led by Captain R.St V. Sherbrooke in HMS *Onslow*. The cruisers *Sheffield* and *Jamaica*, under Rear-Admiral R.L. Burnett, were also in the vicinity. Just as the short winter day was breaking, three of Kummetz's destroyers opened fire on the escort. The convoy turned south under a smokescreen while four of Sherbrooke's destroyers engaged the German attackers on both flanks. The *Sheffield* and the *Jamaica* were diverted at first by a misleading radar contact but finally arrived to engage the *Hipper*. At midday Kummetz gave the order to withdraw and the action came to an end. The British lost a minesweeper and a destroyer, the Germans a destroyer; the *Hipper* had been badly damaged. Hitler was enraged by the failure of the Kriegsmarine to press home this attack when it had had the advantage and he launched such a tirade against Admiral Raeder that the latter had no option but to resign and hand over supreme command to Dönitz. Hitler, who had been notoriously shy of risking his capital ships, even intended them to be paid off, until Dönitz persuaded him to rescind the order early in 1943.

The Shetland air bases expanded their facilities and operations as the war progressed. The second runway at Scatsta beside Sullom Voe became ready in April 1941 and a vast system of underground fuel tanks with a capacity of 225,000 gallons at Graven across the Voe ended local problems with fuel supplies in June. By April 1942 Sumburgh's new runways were big enough to accommodate larger aircraft and sorties were launched to attack targets in Norway. At the same time Catalinas, which had a range of up to 3,500 miles, began to make long patrols far into the Arctic between Jan Mayen and Spitzbergen to detect the edge of the pack ice and the safe routes for convoys.

This type of patrol, to assess meteorological conditions, was carried out by both sides; Sumburgh Hurricanes shot up a Heinkel 111 on weather patrol near Fair Isle in January 1941, causing it to crash land there and committing the three survivors from the five-man crew to captivity. Shetland also became the staging post for long flights to the north of Russia, another route made hazardous by unpredictable weather and problems with fuel consumption. Patrolling aircraft still took homing pigeons aloft with them. When a Whitley VII from 612 Squadron at Wick developed engine and radio trouble in April 1943, causing it to crash land on Foula, 20 miles west of the Shetland Mainland and without a telephone, the crew released their pigeon to inform the base of their plight; as it happened, they were to be rescued by the Aith lifeboat and were back in Wick before the pigeon arrived. In February 1944, however, the pigeon released by a Catalina without fuel and a working radio when it had to touch down on the sea west of Shetland did reach Sullom and alerted the rescue authorities in time to save the crew before the aircraft sank as they were trying to taxi to Ronas Voe.

The patrolling seaplanes began to attack U-boats whenever the opportunity presented itself, one of the first in the north being made by a Walrus from Sullom on Christmas Eve 1940. The U-boat appears to have escaped on that occasion, as did *U-606* when she was depth-charged by a Catalina of the Norwegian 330 Squadron on 21 September 1942. Operating from Akureyri, the Norwegians spotted the U-boat trailing convoy QP14 on the surface north-east of Jan Mayen. Anti-aircraft fire from *U-606* struck the Catalina wounding two crewmen and puncturing the fuel tanks. *U-606* escaped the Catalina's depth charges and got away. The Catalina was forced to touch down on the sea near the convoy and the crew were rescued by the destroyer *Marne*. Two days later, a Catalina crew from 210 Squadron at Sullom chalked up that base's first U-boat kill when they sank *U-253* north-east of Iceland.

In the summer of 1942 the Shetland Bus became an independent unit within the Royal Norwegian Navy. In the following October Prince Olav, the Crown Prince of Norway, paid an official visit to the Scalloway base of the Shetland Bus where he impressed the Norwegian fishermen who manned the operation. The slipway was named in his honour. David Howarth records, however, that after this happy event in the autumn, the operations of the Bus in the succeeding winter were beset with difficulties. Five boats – the *Aksel*, *Sandöy*, *Feie*, *Brattholm* and *Bergholm* – were lost, along with forty-two men. The *Aksel* went down with all hands on her way home before help could reach her, and the exact cause of her sinking remains unknown. The

Feie disappeared without trace on her outward voyage. German coastal patrols had become more intense and they had learned to be highly suspicious of seemingly innocent fishing boats. The clandestine penetration of the fjords in this way was clearly becoming increasingly dangerous, no matter how brave and skilled the crews, and Howarth and his colleagues came to the conclusion that their day was done. They were nevertheless very reluctant to throw in the towel completely and Howarth began to search for a new type of vessel in which they could carry on. At last, in August 1943, the United States Navy supplied the solution – three submarine chasers, each 110 feet long, with a pair of 1200 horse power diesel engines giving a top speed of 22 knots, and equipped with a superb range of gadgets and gear.

They were renamed the *Hitra*, the *Hessa* and the *Vigra*, and with them the Bus took on a new lease of life. After the crews, twenty-two men on each one, had had their shakedown cruises, the subchasers began operations in the autumn of 1943. The three skippers were Leif Larsen, Petter Salen and Lieutenant Eidsheim of the Royal Norwegian Navy. Boasting an impressive array of weapons, including a forward Bofors gun and two twin Oerlikons in power-operated turrets, they were well able to give a good account of themselves in any scrap with the enemy. Howarth says they were never attacked although German aircraft often flew down to inspect them. Over the winter of 1943–44, they completed thirty-four operations; and in the 1944–45 season, eighty – with no casualties. Howarth concludes his account of the new ships in an almost disappointed tone: 'Work with the subchasers was so successful and so uneventful that it almost took on the nature of a

Fig. 84
The plaque at Scalloway commemorating the visit by Prince Olav in 1942.
(Robert Manson)

Fig. 85
The Shetland Bus plaque at Scalloway.
(Robert Manson)

Fig. 86

The Hitra, *one of the American subchasers donated to the Shetland Bus for operations on the coast of occupied Norway. (Norges Hjemmefront Museum)*

naval patrol, and a detailed chronicle of it would make dull reading.'

Dull it may have been in comparison with the unpredictable adventures that preceded it but the Bus continued to keep contact with the Norwegian mainland open. Overall the Bus made 94 trips with fishing boats and 109 with the subchasers. They landed agents and radio transmitters to provide invaluable intelligence about the enemy, supplied resistance forces with over 400 tons of arms and equipment, and rescued 350 refugees.

The Shetland Bus is the most famous of the operational units that crossed the North Sea to harass or sustain occupied Norway, and its career has tended to overshadow the comparable exploits of other forces. Between 1941 and 1943, the Secret Intelligence Service ran fishing boats from a base at Peterhead to land agents of the Special Operations Executive in Norway and made twenty-three trips before the danger of being found out by the Germans caused SIS to switch to using vessels operating from Shetland.

The Royal Norwegian Navy acquired motor torpedo boats (MTBs) and motor gun boats (MGBs) to form the 30th MTB Flotilla. Powered by four Packard petrol engines, with an overall length of 115 feet and a crew of around thirty officers and men, these vessels, nicknamed 'dog boats' by the

Fig. 87
ML 466 off Shetland in June 1943.
(Copyright IWM, Neale. No. HU 67161A)

Royal Navy, were ideally suited for hit and run raids. Their armament varied but normally included 2-pounder guns, machine guns, Oerlikons, torpedo tubes and depth charges. Rather unglamorously, the boats had numbers rather than names. The 30th Flotilla was formed after an experimental operation in October 1941. The Norwegian destroyer *Draug* to save fuel towed *MTB 56* across to a point outside the Inner Leads south of Bergen and then left Lieutenant Per Danielsen and his crew to see what they could achieve. Danielsen took *MTB 56* into the Inner Leads, lay up for a day under camouflage netting until darkness fell, sank a tanker with torpedoes, dodged the escorts and returned safely with the *Draug* to Lerwick.[70]

The Flotilla operated from Lerwick under Lieutenant Ragnald Tamber, the senior Royal Norwegian Navy officer, with nine boats during 1942 and 1943. Usually two or three MTBs sailed together on missions, timing their crossings to reach the Norwegian coast as darkness fell. Using their local knowledge they were able to navigate in the complex maze of islands and leads, and find suitable hiding places for the daylight hours as they waited for an opportunity to strike at shipping. The range of the boats at maximum speed was around 500 miles and any trip more than the shortest meant they had to carry extra fuel in drums on deck, creating an additional hazard should they be attacked by aircraft. Bad weather, as always, could seriously interfere with any schedule and, like the fishermen on the Shetland Bus, the dog boats had to endure some savage conditions, particularly on their return voyages. *MTB 625* nearly succumbed to a gale in February 1944 off the Norwegian coast when the force of the seas broke her keel: wind speeds of 130 mph were recorded at Sumburgh in that storm and it beggars the imagination to understand how the crew of the MTB managed to steer their vessel home, let alone keep her afloat, until they beached in Shetland. *MTB 666* of the Royal Navy was with *625* on that mission and also succeeded in making it back to the islands.

Early in January 1943, two officers from the Lerwick flotilla disguised themselves as fishermen and crossed in a fishing boat to the island of Stord close to the mouth of Hardangerfjord. As the boat came into harbour German sentries helped it to moor. Hoping their disguise would hold, the officers went ashore to look around – their aim was to carry out a reconnaissance of the layout and defences of the pyrites mines at Sagvåg on the island, a mission they accomplished successfully – before re-embarking and returning to Shetland with their intelligence. On the night of the 23–24 January, seven MTBs set out on the raid. *MTB 618* and *MTB 623* attacked a lookout post north of Stord, and MTBs 620, 625 and 631 penetrated the fjord waters to create general mayhem by setting alight a herring oil plant, firing on shore batteries, laying mines and sinking a cargo boat. These, however, were diversions. The two remaining MTBs, 626 and 627, landed an equally mixed Norwegian–British force of fifty commandos at Sagvåg. Half engaged the German defences in a fierce exchange of fire while the others struggled to the mine with explosives. By the early hours of the morning the raid was over: the mine buildings had been blasted to pieces, the shaft filled with damaged hoisting gear, and the loading plant on the quayside blown up, putting the mine out of action for a year. The raiders suffered only one fatal casualty.

The operations of the 30th Flotilla carried on through the middle years of the war, usually with success. At times, however, a tragic outcome overtook the dog boats. *MTB 345*, a much smaller vessel of a different type from the others in the Flotilla, was captured in July 1943 and her eight-man crew was executed by the Gestapo. *MTB 675* was attacked by aircraft on her way home in October 1943 and badly shot up: she eventually limped back to Scotland on one engine and dead reckoning, arriving at Dunbar in East Lothian, far south of her home port.

In October, in a reorganisation of the Coastal Forces, the 30th Flotilla was re-designated as the 54th. The 58th Flotilla of the Royal Navy, under the command of Lieutenant Commander Ken Gemmell, joined the 54th shortly afterwards. On 22 November, MTBs 626 of the 54th and 686 of the 58th caught fire and blew up while alongside the quay in Lerwick. Exactly how the explosion was set off seems to be unknown but somehow the accidental firing of an Oerlikon set fire to the petrol cans arrayed on the deck of 686. The blaze instantly spread out of control over both MTBs and the ammunition and fuel tanks erupted, blowing both vessels to pieces and killing five men.

The two flotillas collaborated on operations until in March 1944 they were transferred to ports on the east coast of England to assist in the D-Day landings. In September the 54th Flotilla returned to Shetland and Lieutenant Commander Charles Herlofson took over command from Lieutenant Tamber. Raids on shipping in the Inner Leads continued until April 1945 and one of the most remarkable incidents of all happened towards the end of that month. The event began when the captain of *U-637*, expecting assistance as his electrical system was faulty, mistook the Norwegian MTBs *711* and *723*, on their way home after lying in the Inner Leads, for German naval units and surfaced his vessel beside them. The Norwegians recovered from their surprise and let loose torpedoes. These missed, and a close-range gun battle developed, the protagonists dodging around each other trying to gain advantage. The fight attracted the attention of shore batteries and the MTBs, their ammunition almost exhausted, decided to withdraw. The German seamen managed to bring the crippled, shot-up U-boat into port but several of her crew and her captain had been killed and she was never repaired.

The Battle of the North Cape, fought between Home Fleet units from Scapa Flow, led by Admiral Sir Bruce Fraser in HMS *Duke of York*, and the battle-cruiser *Scharnhorst*, commanded by Rear-Admiral Erich Bey, on 26 December 1943 ended with the sinking of the latter and the removal of a major threat to the Arctic convoys. Bey's crew fought gallantly to the end and, after she finally sank under the icy waves of the Barents Sea, only thirty-six survivors out of her complement of almost two thousand were fished from the sea. The demise of the *Scharnhorst* left only the battleship *Tirpitz* in the Norwegian fjords. It has been recounted above how the attempt by Leif Larsen's party to attack her with Chariots failed at the outset. On 22 September 1943, only a couple of weeks after the *Tirpitz* had bombarded Spitzbergen, incidentally the only time she seems to have fired her 15-inch guns in anger, midget submarines, the X craft, managed to creep into Altafjord to damage her sufficiently to remove her for a time as a strategic

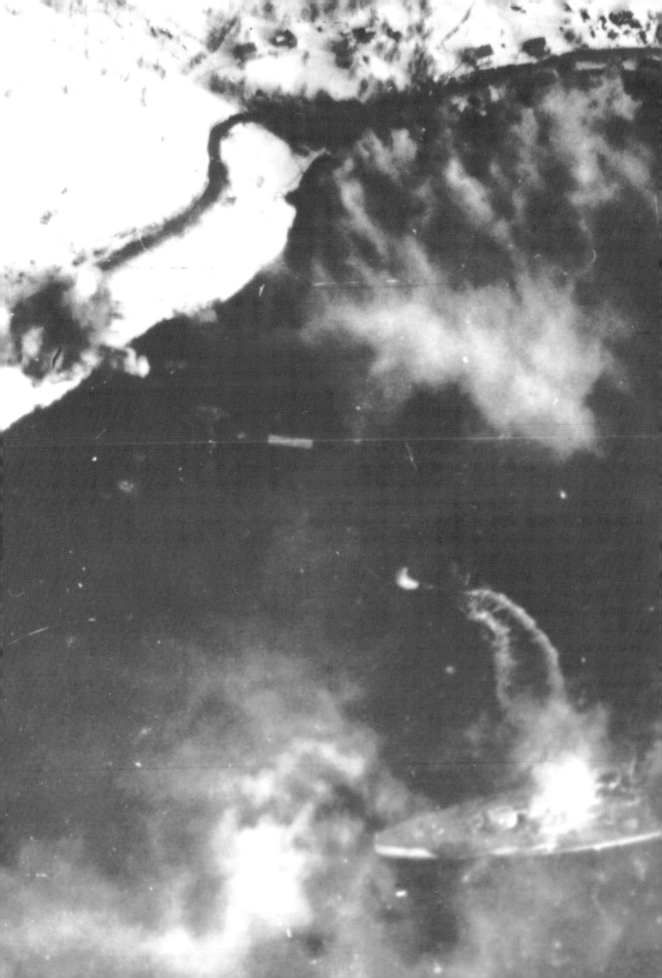

Fig. 88

An airman's view of the Tirpitz *in Altafjord under attack by Barracuda bombers of the Fleet Air Arm on 3 April 1944. The cloud from an exploding bomb billows upward as a motorboat leaves a curling wake beside the battleship's port quarter. (Copyright IWM. No. A 22633)*

threat. The Fleet Air Arm and the RAF then launched several attacks on her but she remained stubbornly afloat. RAF Lancasters, capable of dropping 12,000-lb bombs, damaged her in September 1944 and she was moved to Tromsø for repair. A second attack by Lancasters, on 12 November, finally achieved success, causing the great ship to capsize at her moorings with a heavy loss of life.

Through 1944 the Allies gradually achieved ascendancy over the U-boat threat. August 1943, when U-boats managed to sink only a handful of ships, turned out to be the lowest ebb in Dönitz's campaign to dent the trans-atlantic trade and thereafter losses in the convoys increased again but never reached the levels of 1942. Air power in the form of constant patrolling of the Bay of Biscay and the Shetland–Iceland gap dealt with many U-boats, as the Kriegsmarine tried to reinforce its units in the Biscay area by diverting vessels from the far north. In the latter half of May, Coastal Command sank six out of twenty-two U-boats sighted in northern waters, and there were a further seven kills overall in June. U-boats, however, were hardly sitting ducks. They could throw up a fierce anti-aircraft fire and frequently preferred to stay on the surface to fight it out with a single attacker from the sky.

In all, in the last sixteen months of the war, aircraft from Sullom accounted for at least eight U-boats. Since not every attack resulted in a confirmed kill, the number could be higher. One of the first, *U-601*, was detected and depth-charged by a Catalina from 210 Squadron on 25 February 1944, and became the first U-boat to be sunk inside the Arctic Circle. On 24 May a Sunderland from 422 Squadron of the Royal Canadian Air Force was brought down by *U-921*. Later that same day another Sunderland, this time from 423 Squadron, found *U-921* on the surface but again the submarine escaped; her skipper, Oberleutnant Wolfgang Leu, enabled an unusually rapid crash dive by staying on deck himself so he could close the hatch from the outside, saving his ship and his crew but ensuring his own death.

On 17 July Flying Officer John Cruickshanks of 210 Squadron won the Victoria Cross for his bravery after an attack on *U-361*.[71] Cruickshanks was piloting his Catalina on a fourteen-hour patrol from Sullom when, west of Lofoten, the radar picked up the U-boat on the surface. In the first attack the depth charges failed to release. On the second they fell away to straddle the U-boat but in the meantime *U-361*'s gunfire had raked the Catalina, killing the navigator and wounding four other men, including the co-pilot and Cruickshanks. Cruickshanks collapsed but recovered and took over the controls again until the aircraft was on course for home. Refusing morphine in case it impaired his ability to carry on, Cruickshanks and the less experienced co-pilot flew the aircraft for five hours to get back to Sullom and circled for another hour until the light improved enough for the crippled Catalina to touch down and beach safely. Cruickshanks turned out to have been struck in seventy-two places and had lost so much blood he had to have a transfusion before leaving the aircraft. *U-361* was later confirmed to have been sunk.

As the Allies gradually prevailed during 1944 and 1945, German forces retreated on all fronts. The withdrawal from the north of Norway was accompanied by a scorched-earth policy and civilians had to be evacuated from Söröya and Svalbard by the Shetland Bus. The war-effort in the northern islands was now winding down – the RAF had closed its Vágar base in the Faroes on 1 September, and the Shetland Home Guard had held their last parade at Fort Charlotte on 3 December – but the weeks were still marked by some notable incidents. The *Empire Unity*, a tanker in convoy RU161, the third last convoy in the series, was torpedoed on 4 May in Faxafloi, the large bight on the Icelandic coast off Reykjavik. The crew were picked up by the trawler *Northern Spray*. Three hours later, the tanker was still afloat and Lieutenant Geoffrey Thorpe in command of the *Northern Spray* decided to try to salvage her, despite the risk of another attack and the deteriorating weather. Robert Everett, the *Empire Unity*'s chief engineer, recruited five volunteers from her crew and, with some seamen from the trawler, led by George Lawson, went alongside the tanker and scrambled aboard. The tanker was in ballast but she was listing 15 degrees and the gases in her empty tanks carried the risk of explosion. The salvage crew, however, got her under way and brought her safely into Hvalfjord.[72]

On 4 May 1945, the German forces in north-western Europe, including Denmark, surrendered to the Allies and this joyful news reached the Faroes late that evening. There was naturally great jubilation and the people filled the streets in Thorshavn. The telegram service to Denmark re-opened on Monday the 7th and a cable arrived from the liberated Danish government to thank Mr Hilbert, the *amtmand*, for all his good work. As a reminder, however, that the enemy in Norway had not yet surrendered, a Luftwaffe aircraft attacked a Faroese fishing boat on the same day – without doing harm. The war in Europe came publicly and completely to an end at midnight on VE Day – Tuesday 8 May 1945.

Now, with the end of the war in Europe, the *Shetland Times* noted 'the mood was one of thankfulness and restrained joy' before going on to remind its readers, although few would have needed to be told, that men from the islands were still not safely home but at sea or somewhere in Europe, where they had sustained heavy casualties.[73] As elsewhere, flags sprouted on buildings and ships, and there was a general explosion of noise from church bells, sirens and rockets. A small crowd assembled by the Market Cross in Lerwick to talk and dance. The kirks stayed open for private prayer and plans were put into action for more formal services of thanksgiving. There was a similar, somewhat muted reaction in Kirkwall; Orkney's 226 anti-aircraft battery was still engaged against the Japanese in Burma.

In Iceland there was a riot. It was as if all the pent-up annoyance of the Icelanders at having had to host foreign troops for four years, and all the frustration of the servicemen at having to stay in such a place, was released in a massive punch-up. One Admiralty report on the fighting refers to high spirits, heavy drinking and some Iceland 'rowdies … itching for a scrap'.[74] How exactly it started remains obscure but obviously the first spark needed very little tinder. The trouble probably began when a merchant seaman ventured to drape a White Ensign on the statue of the city's founder, Ingólfur Arnason. The Icelanders resented this desecration and youngsters began to throw stones, or the White Ensign may have been hauled down and trampled on. A brawl broke out and bottles, stones, clubs, even coal, became weapons. Gerald Shepherd, the British minister, noted that the men of the Royal Norwegian Navy fought alongside the Royal Navy and the Merchant Marine. The Reykjavik fire tender tried to cow the rioters but was forced to retreat with a broken windscreen. Military police from the Navy, the Marines and the RAF were called in to assist the Icelandic police; two of the RAF police had to be hospitalised. At last the RAF Assistant Provost Marshall and the Chief of Police decided to use tear gas to quell the mayhem. Reports of fatalities were soon discredited. There was further, although brief, fighting on the following day and on the 10th all British officers and ratings were ordered to stay in their barracks. Strangely the outburst seemed to have cleared the air, for on the 14th it was reported that there was no resultant local ill feeling. The Chief of Police thought that both sides were equally to blame. Early accounts of the riots were dismissed as greatly exaggerated and partly blamed by the British on Lieutenant-Colonel D. Hjalmarrsson, head of US Counter Intelligence, who was of Icelandic origin and, according to the Royal Navy, 'violently anti-British'.

In the wake of the riots, the Admiralty refused to consider a request from the ACIC, Rear-Admiral B.C.Watson, and the British minister, Gerald Shepherd, to donate radio beacons to the Iceland government as compensation for the damage wrought by the rampaging seamen, and ordered that they be sold instead.[75]

On 7 May a Sunderland from 210 Squadron at Sullom Voe sank *U-320*,

Fig. 89
*Reykjavik harbour,
looking NNE.
(Copyright PRO)*

REYKJAVIK HARBOUR, facing NNE.

Fig. 90

The Royal Navy base at
Hvitanes, Iceland, in
1943, commissioned as
HMS Baldur III.
(Copyright PRO)

the last U-boat kill of the war. On the same day, another Sullom Sunderland, this time from 330 Squadron, picked up some important passengers and flew with them to Oslo, the first Norwegian aircraft to return home. The German troops in Norway had surrendered on 6 May. The three subchasers of the Shetland Bus and the MTBs from Lerwick sailed in triumph into a liberated homeland; 330 Squadron had their last parade at Sullom Voe on 29 May, and soon thereafter operations wound down almost to zero. Coastal Command also closed down its activity at Sumburgh. *U-532*, with cargo from Japan, surfaced near the Faroes to surrender on 10 May, and the Norwegian destroyer *Stord* accepted the surrender of fifteen more U-boats in Vestfjord on the 16th. By the end of May twelve U-boats had made their way to Scapa Flow to surrender; later *U-776* was to be open to the public in Kirkwall and Lerwick. Early in June the postal service to Norway resumed. When the surrender of Japan signalled the end of the War, the lights went on again in Lerwick and celebrating crowds filled the streets.

The occupation of the Faroes and Iceland had a major economic and constitutional impact on these two countries. On 25 April 1940, Britain had announced to the Faroese through the BBC that all their ships should fly the flag of the Faroese independence movement rather than the Danish flag, a shift of colours originally proposed by most of the parties in the Løgting, although opposed by the *amtmand* and the Unionists. The war opened up a major new market for Faroese fish and for their international seaborne trade, for the Faroese took on the task of sailing to Britain with not only their own catches but fish from Iceland as well. More than one fifth of British fish landings during the war were brought to harbour by Faroese vessels and, of course, the islands benefited financially, their sterling balances rising from £248,000 in January 1941 to £2,792,000 in July 1945.[76] There was also a price to pay – four trawlers, six sloops and fifteen schooners were lost, with a total of 132 hands. Most fell victim to air attack and the Royal Navy began to issue machine guns to the fishing boats in April 1941; they claimed one enemy aircraft, a Heinkel, early in 1942, shot down by a boat skipper from Sandavágur, an act for which he was awarded an MBE.

The five-year taste of home rule gave the Faroese an increased appetite for independence. In December 1945 the Løgting sent a delegation to Copenhagen to open talks on constitutional change. These led to a referendum in September 1946 which produced a very narrow majority in favour of self-government; this result was not well received in Denmark and attempts were made to thwart Faroese wishes, moves that only made the islanders the more determined to see the matter through. Finally on 1 April

1948 the Faroes became a self-governing community but with some powers, for example, defence, reserved to Denmark.

   Iceland went sooner and further in its pursuit of complete independence from Denmark. The country already enjoyed a considerable measure of self-government, to all intents and purposes a sovereign state since 1918 but retaining the Danish monarch as head of state. The War had prevented a review of this arrangement scheduled to have taken place in 1940, and in 1941 the *Althing* declared that Iceland had gained the right to full independence. A plebiscite in 1944 approved of the proposal to form a republic and on 17 June that year the republic officially came into being, the announcement being made appropriately at Thingvellir on the historic, open-air site of the island's ancient parliament, the oldest in Europe. King Christian X cabled his good wishes. Sveinn Björnsson passed from being his country's regent to being its first president. The new republic reminded the world of its independence by declining to declare for the Allies and calling for the immediate withdrawal of the occupying forces as soon as hostilities ceased.

   Like the Faroes, Iceland had done well in economic terms. The foreign troops, especially the free-spending Americans, had amounted at times to one third of the population and had invested considerable sums in infrastructure,

Fig. 91

The Faroese freighter the Smiril leaves Trangisvåg-fjord on 12 October 1942 on another voyage to bring essential supplies to the islands. Her flag and nationality are painted on her side to identify her and emphasise her protected status, but she was attacked several times by the Luftwaffe. (Copyright IWM, Neale. No. HU 67157)

Fig. 92

A cartoon showing how the Churchill Causeways, or barriers, stopped any U-boat incursions into Scapa Flow. The first image shows HMS Royal Oak at anchor. The signature belongs to A V Alexander, the First Lord of the Admiralty, who came up to Orkney to declare the Causeways formally open. (Orkney Library)

including the airfield at Keflavik, as well as in general trade. It was estimated that military spending had amounted to almost £23,000,000 and that wage rates for labour had risen by as much as 400 per cent.[77] In the middle of the War, around 3,000 Icelanders found work on Allied construction projects. The Icelandic national income rose by 60 per cent and the trading of fish to Britain and especially to America brought in currency and consumer goods. There had been problems with rising prices, as well as housing and labour shortages – 250 Faroese had been recruited to work in Iceland in the summer of 1941 – and strikes had flared up; but these were years also of opportunity. As for the Faroes, there had been losses: at least four fishing trawlers, as well as the steamer *Hekla*, torpedoed en route to America in September 1941, and in all 352 Icelandic seamen and fishermen had lost their lives.

Orkney and Shetland could also tot up the credit and debit of war. Farm produce and livestock found a ready market as in the First World War, and there was considerable building of infrastructure that would stand the islanders in good stead in the years to come. The islands on the east side of Scapa Flow, for example, were now connected to the Mainland by a series of causeways, popularly referred to as the Churchill Barriers, built at a cost that would probably have defied peacetime investment.

Some wartime conditions persisted for too long in the islanders' view. A

Fig. 93

A naval gun on the breastwork of Skansin fort in Thorshavn, looking south towards the island of Nolsoy and the southern approach to the Faroese capital. (author)

few restrictions on civilian freedom stayed in place – every adult still had to carry an identity card, and it was still forbidden to use a telescope or binoculars in public. The *Shetland Times* protested on 20 July:

> With Orkney, Shetland is now the only regulated area in the United Kingdom. The regulations are not irksome and indeed hardly touch the life of the average person. For over five years the inhabitants have had to thole many restrictions on their normal activities and have borne them as part of the common effort … Yet is it not curious that the Authorities quickly discover the importance of these remote parts when strategic needs prove vital, and appear to shelve them when ordinary affairs are being considered?

It was just a matter of time. On 1 August 1945, the Scalloway base of the Shetland Bus officially closed. In September French workers arrived to dismantle Navy huts at Lyness on Hoy and ship them home where they were needed for housing, and the naval base in Lerwick, HMS *Fox*, closed at the end of that month. Gradually the troops disappeared and gradually the islanders' own service people came home. Bit by bit, peacetime conditions returned to the northern lands, although the war still had a sting in its tail:

Fig. 94

*The Faroese war
memorial in Thorshavn.*
(author)

on a Friday morning in November a sea mine drifted ashore to explode in South Braewick and blew the door off a nearby crofthouse. In December the Royal Navy headquarters in Kirkwall closed its doors. ENSA staged its last show at the Garrison Theatre in Stromness on 24 January 1946, and the garrison in Shetland finally closed on 29 March.

During the Cold War the northern islands found themselves once again in the front line, facing the route Soviet submarines had to take to reach the Atlantic. Iceland was reluctantly persuaded to relinquish its preferred policy of neutrality and join NATO in 1949, and became the site of a large military base at Keflavik. A radar station was established in the Faroes, and a number of defence installations were placed in Shetland – at Saxa Vord, Collafirth, Mossy Hill and Sumburgh. Scapa Flow remained a naval base until 1957 but still found a role thereafter in NATO exercises.

The Cold War itself has now ended and, in turn, some of the military bases associated with it have been reduced in size. One positive side-effect of the Second World War has been the rediscovery by the northern islanders of the historic and cultural ties that bind them and mainland Scandinavia, and this is a legacy that will probably endure. The collective memory will hold on to the grim time when the islands themselves marked a front line in the great struggles in European history.

REFERENCES AND NOTES

Many books have been written about naval events in the two World Wars. A few are listed in the Bibliography, and more particular references to sources used in this book are given below. The abbreviations ADM, WO and AIR refer to Admiralty, War Office (Army) and Air (RAF) files respectively in the Public Record Office Kew, London.

1. West.
2. *Shetland Times*, 30 July 1904.
3. *Shetland Times*, 17 Sept 1904.
4. ADM 116/1293.
5. See, for example, Miller and Hewison.
6. Ranft.
7. *The Times*, repeated in *Orkney Herald*, 17 Sept 1919.
8. Patterson.
9. Patterson.
10. Chatterton and Hampshire provide comprehensive histories of the Northern Patrol. A draft of the official history by Lt Cdr A.C. Bell is available in ADMs 116/3304 to 116/3308.
11. *Shetland Times*, 8 Aug 1914.
12. Alston. See note 23.
13. Pulling.
14. Charles Sandison, 'A famous Unst ketch: the *Silver Lining*', *New Shetlander*, No. 65, 1963.
15. *Orkney Herald*, 15 Aug 1906.
16. Farago gives a comprehensive history of German espionage in Britain.
17. Mackay and Manson provide detailed accounts of the Lerwick Post Office affair.
18. Chatterton.
19. Some details of the *Oceanic* wreck are taken from *Shetland Times*, 12 Sept 1914. Other information is from a memoir by William Mann in the Shetland Archives (WMNS 77).

20. Shetland Archives (JAMNS 182).

21. The quote is from W.B. Hayle's book *American Rights and British Pretensions on the Seas,* and is given in Chatterton.

22. *My Life at Sea*, Captain Hoseason's memoir, Shetland Archives (Caphosea).

23. Captain Alston's memoir, *Shetland in the Last War*, Shetland Archives (Alston). Also serialised in the *Shetland News* from 14 Dec 1939.

24. Lena N. Mouat, 'With the WRNS 1914–18.', *New Shetlander*, No. 107, 1974.

25. Fisher's memorandum is quoted in Patterson.

26. Information from Shetland Museum.

27. Alston. See note 23.

28. ADM 137/3649.

29. ADM 137/3627.

30. McRobb.

31. Captain Robert Manson's unpublished memoir, here paraphrased.

32. ADM 137/3744.

33. Messimer and Hoehling provide accounts of the North Sea Barrage.

34. *Orkney Herald*, 13 Nov 1918.

35. Barbara Ann Black's *The Impact of External Shocks upon a Peripheral Economy: War and Oil in Twentieth Century Shetland* (PhD Thesis, University of Glasgow, 1995) has much useful data.

36. Tulloch.

37. The story of the internment, scuttling and subsequent salvage of much of the German High Seas Fleet is given in Miller, Hewison and George.

38. Ship biographies of US Navy vessels are given in the *Dictionary of American Naval Fighting Ships,* available on website www.hazegray.org/danfs. There is also a short account of the sweeping of the Barrage in Hewison.

39. ADM 116/4252.

40. *Shetland News*, 18 Nov 1939. This bombing raid is said to have inspired the wartime hit song 'Run Rabbit Run'.

41. Sims.

42. David Hanson's comprehensive 'Shetland Crash Log' gives details of air warfare incidents. I was able to access an unpublished copy, but it has been serialised in *Aviation Archaeologist*, 2nd Series, Nos. 18–23.

43. ADM 1/10739.

44. ADM 1/10739 is the main official source on the occupation of the Faroes. There is also useful information in Dam, West and WO 193/758.

45. The rather unlikely note that some Icelanders were favourable to joining the British Empire appears in a report dated 25 March 1940 in ADM 1/10739. This file, with ADM 199/671 and ADM 199/672, are the main sources on the occupation of Iceland.

46. *Orcadian*, 7 Dec 1939.

47. *Orkney View*, No. 30, 1990.

48. *Orkney View*, No. 40, 1992.

49. Professor Magne Skodvin's article summarises the story of the Shetland Bus. A detailed Norwegian history is given in Ragnar Ulstein's *Englandsfarten*, Oslo 1965–67.

50. Howarth. After the war, Howarth's book *The Shetland Bus* became a bestseller and was made into a film. The book has recently been reissued with new material.

51. Melville.

52. WO 193/758.

53. Linklater, 1970.

54. Linklater, 1941.

55. Whitehead.

56. Linklater, 1970.

57. Information from Sandes, E.W.C. *From Pyramid to Pagoda*, the official history of the West Yorkshire Regiment, from the Prince of Wales's Own Regiment of Yorkshire, York.

58. Churchill, Vol. II.

59. Whitehead.

60. General reports from the Admiral Commanding Iceland are in ADM 199/671.

61. Morison, Vol. I.

62. Churchill, Vol. III.

63. ADM 199/2112.

64. WO 193/758.

65. AIR 15/322.

66. AIR 28/873.

67. Information on the experiences of the Cameronians and the South Staffordshire Regiment, including extracts from Kenneth Macmillan, *A Brief History of the 12th Battalion The Cameronians (Scottish Rifles) June 1940–November 1943*, was provided by the respective regimental museums.

68. Hanson (see Note 41) and Lamb summarise air accidents in Shetland and Orkney respectively.

69. ADM 1/11153.

70. Reynolds gives a comprehensive account of MTB and MGB operations in northern waters.
71. The U-boat attacked by Cruickshanks and his crew is frequently named as *U-347* but Franks and Zimmerman have recently presented evidence for it having been *U-361*.
72. ADM 1/30683.
73. *Shetland Times*, 11 May 1945.
74. ADM 1/18285 has reports on the Reykjavik riots.
75. ADM1/18285.
76. West.
77. Chamberlin.

BIBLIOGRAPHY

Chadwick, F. *Gash Boat: HMS Coventry 1939–1942*. Stornoway, 1999

Chamberlin, W.C. *Economic Development of Iceland Through World War II*, New York, 1968

Chatterton, E. Keble. *The Big Blockade*, London, 1932

Churchill, W.S. *The Second World War*, 6 vols. London, 1948–54

Dam, F.H. 'The British occupation of the Faroe Islands 1940–1945', *British Army Review*, April 1990

Derry, T.K. *A History of Scandinavia*, London, 1979

Farago, Ladislas. *The Game of the Foxes*, London, 1971

Fitzpatrick, T.A. *Weather and War*, Durham, 1992

Franks, N. and Zimmerman E., *U-Boat versus Aircraft*, London, 1998

George, S.C. *Jutland to Junkyard*, London, 1973; reissued Edinburgh 1999

Gunn, Simon. 'The Catfirth Flying Boat Station', *New Shetlander*, No. 139, 1982

Hampshire, A. Cecil. *The Blockaders*, London, 1980

Hewison, W.S. *This Great Harbour: Scapa Flow*, Kirkwall, 1985

HMSO. *The Battle of the Atlantic*, London, 1946

HMSO. *Combined Operations 1940–1942*, London, 1943

Hoehling, A.A. *The Great War at Sea*, London, 1965

Howarth, David. *The Shetland Bus*, London, 1951; reissued Lerwick, 2000

Hough, Richard. *The Great War at Sea 1914–1918*, Edinburgh, 2000

Irvine, J.W. *Lerwick*, Lerwick, 1985

Irvine, J.W. *The Waves Are Free: Shetland/ Norway Links 1940–1945*, Lerwick, 1988

Irvine, J.W. *The Giving Years: Shetland and Shetlanders 1939–1945*, Lerwick, 1991

Lamb, Gregor. *Sky over Scapa, 1939–1945*, Birsay, Orkney, 1991.

Linklater, Eric. *The Northern Garrisons*. London, 1941

Linklater, Eric. *Fanfare for a Tin Hat*, London, 1970

Mackay, J.A. *Islands Postal History. Series No. 8: Shetland*, Dumfries, 1979

McRobb, A.W. *The North Boats: the story of the North of Scotland, Orkney and Shetland Shipping Company,* Narbeth, Pembrokeshire, 1999

Manson, J.H. 'The Lerwick Post Office Arrest', *Shetland Life,* August 2001

Melville, M.L. *The Story of the Lovat Scouts,* Edinburgh, 1981

Messimer, Dwight R. *Find and Destroy: Antisubmarine Warfare in World War I,* Annapolis, MD, 2001

Miller, James. *Scapa,* Edinburgh, 2000

Morison, Samuel E. *The Battle of the Atlantic: History of US Naval Operations in World War II,* Vol. 1, Boston, 1955

Morison, Samuel E. *The Atlantic Battle Won: History of US Naval Operations in World War II,* Vol. X, London, 1956

Patterson, A.T. (ed.) *The Jellicoe Papers Vol. 1: 1893–1916,* London, 1964

Pulling, A. (ed.) *Defence of the Realm Manual,* London, 1918

Ranft, B.M. (ed.) *The Beatty Papers, Vol 1: 1902–1918,* London, 1989

Reynolds, L.C. *Dog Boats at War,* London, 1998

Roskill, S.W. *The Navy at War 1939–1945,* London, 1960

Schei, L.K. & G. Moberg. *The Faroe Islands,* London, 1991

Sims, G. *HMS Coventry: Anti-Aircraft Cruiser,* London, 1972

Skodvin, M. 'Shetland and Norway in the Second World War' in *Shetland and the Outside World 1469–1969,* ed. D.J. Withrington, Oxford, 1983

Smith, David J. *Action Stations: 7: Military Airfields of Scotland, the North-East and Northern Ireland,* Wellingborough, 1989

Tulloch, Peter A. *A Window on North Ronaldsay,* Kirkwall, 1974.

Vat, Dan van der. *The Atlantic Campaign,* London 1988; reissued Edinburgh, 2001

Ward, Peter. *Sullom Voe and Scatsta,* Airfield Focus No. 13, Peterborough, 1994

West, John F. *Faroe: The Emergence of a Nation,* London, 1972

Whitehead A.P. *Harder than Hammers,* London, 1947

Fig. 95 (half-title and overleaf)

Surrendered U-boats gathering in Loch Eriboll at the end of hostilities in 1945. (Orkney Library, Lamb Collection)